T0000505

Phantom Pain Wings

Also by Kim Hyesoon

A Drink of Red Mirror
Autobiography of Death
All the Garbage of the World, Unite!
I'm OK, I'm Pig!
Mommy Must Be a Fountain of Feathers
Poor Love Machine
Sorrowtoothpaste Mirrorcream
When the Plug Gets Unplugged
Princess Abandoned
Anxiety of Words: Contemporary Poetry by Korean Women:
*   Ch'oe Sŭng-ja, Kim Hyesoon, Yi Yŏn-ju*

Phantom Pain Wings

날개 환상통

Kim Hyesoon

Translated from the Korean by Don Mee Choi

A New Directions Paperbook Original

Copyright © 2019 by Kim Hyesoon
Translation and Translator's Diary copyright © 2023 by Don Mee Choi

All rights reserved. Except for brief passages quoted in a newspaper, magazine, radio, television, or website review, no part of this book may be reproduced in any form or by any means, electronic or mechanical, including photocopying and recording, or by any information storage and retrieval system, without permission in writing from the Publisher.

Originally published as 날개 환상통 [*Nalgae hwansangt'ong*] by Moonji Publishing [Munhak gwa jisung sa] in 2019.

The publisher would like to thank Fi Jae Lee for permission to use her drawings. Copyright © 2023 by Fi Jae Lee.

The publication of this book was supported by a grant from the Literature Translation Institute of Korea (LTI Korea).

LTI Korea
Literature Translation Institute of Korea

Manufactured in the United States of America
First published as a New Directions Paperbook (NDP1563) in 2023
Design by Marian Bantjes

Library of Congress Control Number: 2023001719

10 9 8 7 6 5 4 3 2

New Directions Books are published for James Laughlin
by New Directions Publishing Corporation
80 Eighth Avenue, New York 10011

ndbooks.com

Contents

COMMUNITY OF PARTING

WHY DO WOMEN THINK THAT ANIMALS CAN SPEAK?

MY BELOVED PARTING

Bird's Poetry Book

This book is not really a book
It's an I-do-bird sequence
a record of the sequence

When I take off my shoes, stand on the railing
and spread my arms with eyes closed
feathers poke out of my sleeves
Bird-cries-out-from-me-day record
I-do-bird-day record
as I caress bird's cheeks

Air is saturated with wounds
Beneath the wounds matted over me
bird's cheekbones are viciously pointed
yet its bones crack easily when gripped
The birth sequence of such a tiny bird

Poetry ignores
the I-do-bird-woman sequence

Woman-is-dying-but-bird-is-getting-bigger sequence
She says, The pain is killing me
When my hands are tied and my skirt rips like wings
I can finally fly
I was always able to fly like this
Suddenly she lifts her feet
Translation-of-a-certain-bird's-chirping record
of I-do-bird-below-the-railing
sequence

Night's carcass bloats
Waves of tormented spirits
One bird

All the nights of the world
Bird-carrying-the-night's-nipple-
over-the-pointed-as-an-awl-Mount-Everest sequence

Bird with dark eyes has shrunken
Bird has shrunken enough to be cupped in my hands
Bird mumbles something incomprehensible even when my lips touch its
        beak
Bird's tongue is as delicate as a bud
as thin as the tongue of a fetus
The tiny bird's
kicks-off-the-blanket-kicks-my-body-
kicks-the-dirt-and-exits sequence

I end up doing I-do-bird even if I resist doing it
I end up saying this is not a book of poems but a bird

I'll overcome this existence
Finally I'll be free of it

Bird-flies-out-of-water-shaking-its-wings poetry book

Now scribbles of Time's footsteps appear in the book

Scribbles left by skinny bird legs
made with the world's heaviest pencil

Perhaps there's a will left in the scribbles

This book is about the realization of
I-thought-bird-was-part-of-me-but-I-was-part-of-bird sequence
It's a delayed record of such a sequence

The promise of being freed from the book and
being able to step off the paper-thin railing
if I write everything down
It's the delayed record of my regret

Going Going Gone

Bird cuts me out
like the way sunlight cuts out shadows

Hole enters
the spot where I was cut out
I exit

Bird cuts me out
like the way time cuts me

Gaping mouth enters
the cutout

I exit through the open mouth
then return as a deformed child

I exit again

I take a step toward where I don't exist

I take a step toward where I don't exist

Bird doesn't cut me out
Behind the wall I'm on standby forever

Double S
Double S

Ssity doesn't want to know—your mind
Ssity doesn't want to know—your ssorrow

Ssity doesn't want to know anything
yet it offers me sseveral numbers

I'll no longer take up any sspace in this ssity
I'll no longer eat anything

I'll pick a clam with my lips as if I had a beak
ssmudge fish blood onto my face and
grab the wrists of the wind in two equal sstrands

I'll laugh
I'll evaporate
I'll retire

I'll sstay inconspicuous

How long have I walked? When I chewchew the arcade—ice cream sshop,
        bakery, bookstore, noodle sshop—
it feels as if the sscorching ssandy beach is about to pour out from my
        throat

I'll now become a long trail of birds
I'll sswaddle the ssity
then the flock of birds will sspeak

(Next, please draw lines to match ssimilar words)

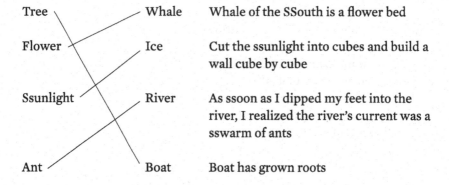

Tree	Whale	Whale of the SSouth is a flower bed
Flower	Ice	Cut the ssunlight into cubes and build a wall cube by cube
Ssunlight	River	As ssoon as I dipped my feet into the river, I realized the river's current was a sswarm of ants
Ant	Boat	Boat has grown roots

Sstreets make the cars ssit up
then ssuspend them up in the air and
the flock of birds sslides down to the river

When the bird embroiders the dark ssea with a golden thread then
ssnatches up the ssea in its beak, ssoars up, and lets go of it
the ssea currents will sswell over the ssity
Sseawater will leak from between the lines of my notebook

Birds have double *s* dangling from the bottom of their feet
(Bird on the railing of the bridge of Han River
Future on its left foot
Past on its right foot
Less, ness, less, ness, less, ness
Bird waddles by sswaying its butt
and *ss* pile up in my diary)

(In the ssity center, I ssuddenly feel the world is sso ssmall; I become claustrophobic)

Therefore, I draw a line across my notebook

sscribbling
away

Bird never sspeaks to anyone first
Of course, I'm the ssame way
My face will grow feathers
I'll fly away

Phantom Pain Wings

Bird in high heels
walks on asphalt, crying

Mascara drips down
My night feathers are infinitely, infinitely large

Critics tell me,
Condolences are for us
You're too filthy for them

I keep dreaming the same dream
It has the face of a human but
is a bird when it stretches out its limbs
I told you not to cut me off
I keep dreaming the same dream
Inside my bone
bird's transparent pathway
Behind my sunglasses
two black beans on a silver platter

(Can you read dreams with those two beans?)

I can't take any calls at the moment because I'm having a meal
I eat as I walk
I lift my head as I walk
I shit blood as I walk

Its name? Bird
That bird with glass stuck to its abdomen
Bird is chased by wind
Maybe it has sand feathers?

Homeless bird
its tiny shoulders
Bird sticks to glass then vanishes

To be honest, I walk because my armpits flutter
I walk because I'm ashamed of my huge wings
I walk because my bird house is smaller than me

When it rains my soaked hands are infinitely, infinitely large

Bird was on its way to die, to hide
The second it turns around to look at me
it chirps, This is Seoul!
There's no place for me to hide here!

Please push me off the cliff!

Bird swirls in the air like a lonely gaze
Critics say,
Safety can't be guaranteed
We'll hit you when you come in
Bird replies, Please stop talking about me!

Bird is up in the air
after being flung onto the ground

Honestly, this isn't the sound of rain
It's the sound of my high heels pounding the asphalt

Tonight, there's no place for me
to hide except in this bathroom
I'm calmed by the sound of
water streaming from the faucet
I mourn in here

My hand trembles
as I curl up my eyelashes with mascara as if lifting up my black wings

The sound of rain hitting the tiles pushes me off the deep end

Tonight, there's no place for me to put down my poem

Bird's Repetition

All the stories bird tells perched on the treetop are about me
Nothing about the rumors of my lies, my thefts and such but
something ordinary like how I was born and died
Bird talks only about me even when I tell it to stop or change the topic
It's always the same story like the sound of the high heels of the woman,
      walking around in the same pair all her life
This is why I have a bird that I want to break

Like a poet who buys a ream of A4 paper
and crumples the sheets one by one and tosses them
I have a bird I want to break
When I crumple up my poems that are like
the family members inside a mirror in front of me
I can hear the stories of fluttering birds
"You were born and died"
Then I say, You scissormouths
and go buy a paper shredder
to shred every poetry book of mine
But later, when I opened up the shredder
a flock of birds was sitting inside, talking about me as if reading line by line
Moreover, each bird had a different face
and the hens talked about me even while sitting on their eggs
They didn't care to fly off
Instead, they clustered under the peanut tree and talked about me
like peanuts under the ground
So, I said to them, enough of telling the same old story of how I was born
      and died
How about something else?
For instance, how about the fact that I always wear the same high heels
to work and back
but when I'm under the same tree at the same park
I always dance a waltz
And do several movements of embracing the moon
But they replied,

You were born inside bird
Not opposite of that
You died inside bird
Not opposite of that
You were born and died

Smell of Wings

The therapist says

Picture a bird in your mind
What kind of bird is it?

It's small and white
It's weightless and colorless, it seeps in and out of its white surroundings
It's lonely when it flies and anxious when it walks
I need to protect it but
I need to protect it yet
(The mumblings of a rescuer)
It has pink armpits
Milky white bird doesn't necessarily cry milky milky milky

They're all lies, really
White bird who just chirped in front of me like a white handkerchief
is bird that politely sips tea
When I scold it, bird says that it couldn't help itself
because of the attacks against me, the questions about my accountability for
        my insanity, my violent language

Actually, I take up a lot of space
I'm about to become the grave of white bird
Every time bird says it couldn't help itself
I want to fly high up
but I get short of breath because my chest is too big
I feel as if I'll knock someone down when I spread my wings
So to be honest, I've never once spread my wings
Ah, ah, my wings are so big that I'm bird that can never be born

My wings smell like my womb's spit
stench of stinky bird

Behind me (What are you doing?)
the therapist says

Now place the bird inside your breast and hug it

Next day
the therapist says

Picture a bird in your mind
What kind of bird is it?

I'm bird that can be born anywhere
I can even be born through a sweat pore
No matter how transparent a bird, it's embarrassed when its body's too big
so mayflies are probably the least embarrassed among those that fly

Behind me (What are you thinking?)
the therapist says

Now hug the mayfly

Glimmer—You Must

Birds I seeded inside your body feel all lumpy—you must

Your blood is replaced with bird's blood—you must

Every day, your footsteps stompstomp up in the air

Every day, idiotic, stupid you can't find the door to your own body

You who wants to become me became frantic to leave your body—you must

It's a muggy summer, but the ground below feels endlessly distant like
　　autumn

Like the way your throat is parched from thirst

your body's birds combust—you must

Puffs of smoke leak from your lips

and birds that want to perch on my body become hot hot hotter by the day

Bam bam inside your heart's nest

a single beat for each hatchling

The day I glimpse howling birds outside the windows of your lukewarm
　　eyes

The day wings quickly sprout, but they're inside the rock

Like your mommy, your right hand

gently pushes down on your chest filled with birds

You do that to me every day in same position

Birds inside you glimmer—you must

Bird Stood as a Question Mark

After I returned home and opened the door
it felt as if the walls took a few steps, then flew up

My room is covered in Post-its

I lie on the floor and imagine a yellow house
Each child sticks its head out from
each picture-frame-like window

One Post-it flickers
and wind that enters can't exit

Today, a pen stuck in my throat made a sound like a bird crying

Roofs covered in black hair flapped about the windows

Why do I stick all of my feathers onto the roofs instead of letting them fall
       to the ground?
Why do my eggs crack and featherless chicks pop out from them?
Why do you throw the cat you befriended into the river and go on your
       vacation?
If you're so ashamed, why don't you just croak, instead of plucking your
       bloody feathers?

The children's choir sings loudly
and takes a breath, holding it in forever
A giant takes off his dark-blue coat
to cover the children, pushing their heads down
I can still feel the heavy coat in my hands

In my room, I can hear the Post-it stuck on the door of the freezer
       breathing

I speak inside the room covered in yellow Post-its

Over there the day is so long that
in a blink of an eye
over here is already gone

What should I do after I finish plucking all my feathers?

In my room, question marks line up like waterfowl

In my room, the walls bob up and down
like waves in an endless trance

In my room, newly hatched birds riding the currents
stroke their yellow feathers one by one with their beaks

Floor Is Not a Floor

Sparkly silver chains on my ankles
As soon as Mommy hatched, she dressed me in a birdcage

My feet keep sinking into the trampoline night
Like a white aurora the rabbit-shaped shadow dissipates
I bounce into the trampoline night

Whowhenwhyhowwherewhat—
I bounce up facing the inexplicable face
The shiny moonlight on my silver chains
gave birth to Mommy, raised and married her off
then made her have me, and now
turns her into a sick bedridden granny
I stretch my hands out to the moon,
Come out! Come out! I'm going to slap your face

I leave Mommy in hospice and I dance a trampoline dance
I don't go to see Mommy, instead I dance, fighting the moon
My dance slays as I dance
My dance makes loud thumping sounds

Trampoline night
Trampoline mountain
Trampoline forest
Sink-sink-into-the-rabbit-shadow-swamp night
I'll fight them
I'll slay them

I'll seduce the mountain
Look here, drink this
summer's monsoon juice
End-of-heatwave-typhoon slush

I'll offer it to the forest
Look here, drink this
Cool-autumn-rain-mixed-fruit nectar
to seduce the giant who lives in the forest

I want to slay the space between sky and land
I want to slay everyplace except where Mommy is lying

I want to slay the rain falling like a black velvet curtain
I want to slay the geraniums under the drops of moonlight

Why did you let Mommy be born?
And why do you let her die?

I can't take off my birdcage dress
It strangles me more each day

I'm entirely dependent on the floor

Trampoline
Trampoline

Does my dress bring destruction?
Bird wearing birdcage with lace curtains

Jumps
Jumps

Is sorrow choreographing my dance? Or is it anxiety?

Lies begin in the morning
They do hurdles, high jumps
Lies begin at night
They fall over, do forward rolls

My silver anklets clang

They say Earth revolves and rotates
orbiting, swirling like my skirt
so why should Mommy die? Why?

Moonlight soaks me like ink, pocking my whole body
Will death stop if I slay all the moonlight?

I fight still wearing my birdcage
with forest
with mountain
with night

If I slay them all, will Mommy live?

Grief Guitar (Etcetera)

The Swan Lake dance troupe arrives to console a coal mine
The moment I + guitar see the clear shoulder straps cutting into the
        dancers' flesh covered in goosebumps
intense pain rips through us as if it came from outer space

I + guitar (dancers) shake our rusted earrings, our knees touching

Even though we take a pick and scratch each other's tightly wound strings
        just a few times

The city lights flicker out one by one

Our hands land on each other, as on barbed wire, leaving tiny scratch marks
        on our bones

Is it the same when a girl's face is poked with a small hypodermic needle?

I + guitar's (dancers') entwined bodies dissolve like pills in water

I + guitar speak out:
How far have you gone down?
How far have you stretched your legs?
For how many generations have you been sick? From your distant ancestors
        to distant descendants?
How far have you died?

Rhythm is an antigravity detention center, preventing our feet from landing

Swan couple (I + guitar) hovers, our pain hovers, our pain's rhythm hovers
        momentarily

We hover riding the echoes of pain from the mountain across the mine

Sometimes we want to keep our knees locked and float in blood like
      watermelon seeds

Sometimes we want to take a pick and pluck at each other's barbed wire
      fence till all the city lights go out

Swan couple's white tights turn crimson from blood

Farewell First

Bird and bird conversed. They conversed on the treetop, on the rooftop with a lightning rod between them. It was freezing that day. Body was inside a toasty-warm room, crying for no apparent reason. Birds' conversation had no body in it. Birds stared at each other like two hands that fell from my body.

Bird begins with farewell first, so what do farewell and farewell talk about when they meet? Bird once started trembling inside my body. Bird may have even fluttered. Bird said, Future doesn't exist since farewell has already begun. Bird and bird pecked on Future and conversed amiably.

The monk who had attained nirvana was always beneath the same tree, and bird always perched on the head of the same monk.

Bird and body said they knew about each other's existence. The day I was so sick, I saw one bird falling from the sky.

Body said that sometimes it can feel bird's visit. Today, bird took my body to the darkest canyon. Body screamed silently, broke into a cold sweat, and flash opened its eyes. Bird left.

On Friday night, traffic came to a halt, so I was stuck in my car on the bridge over the Han River. After the eye surgery, Mommy was alone in bed, her eyes bandaged. Bird flew over to her first and stroked her eyelids.

At that moment, Mommy said she had called out my name.

Girl, Your Body Has So Many Holes for Straws

At night black-and-white keyboards mix wildly
Twilight hour like when the blind stare at the sun
I + bird (tied up with a piano string) + music escape from time

and go up the chimney of white beard's piano repair shop

Girl, how wonderful that there's music playing nonstop in the universe!
says white beard

Things that crossed I + bird + music's minds while flying!
People down there work so hard making stuff their whole life, then they
              pass away
What are they making anyway?
They can't even launch a single star into space
All they do is cook
wash vegetables
make wheels and
write fan letters to pop singers

I + bird + music
create a universe the size of a bathtub
Splash!
Then
I + bird + music float up
like bird's transparent death note

Who keeps erasing our bird house up in the air?

A country where nothing gets wet even if it rains
A country without daddies even if daddies arrive

Pianos tightly strung with nerves
have bad toothaches

But I + bird + music say,
This letter is written by our achy hands
we open the endless letter in the distant future

In the desert
rain falls for the first time in 300 years
The seed that had been waiting for it
shoots up to the very tip of the sky

This infinitely sad, distant scenery
a rain-soaked desert, viewed from a telescope
a lone piano

but it's time, for the thunderous applause to fade
for the cymbals of silence to crash, to announce time's funeral
for Gliese 581c to open its clenched fists and spread gravity's fingers
200 trillion kilometers away

I + bird + music lie prostrate like a corpse, hiding at the bottom of a lake, then
stand up to shake off water, then lie on a bed of shredded radish and fried
glass noodles like a sliced raw fish, panting for air, wearing apricot blossoms
behind our ears, then like strewn laundry fall onto the couch barely breathing,
then do stuff like cooking, washing vegetables, dragging our chained feet,
bleeding.

I + bird + music vomit what we've chomped down, the hour of departure is
          bound to
return, the hour of long-haired tadpoles leaping into frog's dream is bound
          to return.

White beard is bound to jabber away
Girl, your body has so many holes for straws

But it's time to bang on the black-and-white keyboards then a
cool splash! It's time to untie the birds strung to the piano

10 Centimeters

Angel gets locked up now and then
for insanity

I write that I sit on someone else's egg

In black, I scribble all over the pages of the dictionary
I write, sitting inside a birdcage

I can tell when I hold your hand that
you're not a bird
You stick out your dirty hand

When the guard arrives, I hide my tongue inside the thick book

I write,
One morning, I flew up high
One morning, I plunged deep down
I write,
I'll take off when I want to
I write with my beak at the crack of dawn

I fly then stop
I fly then chirp
Inside my made-up world, I can go very far
Not a song
not an echo
but a faraway place where there's only freedom
I'm bird, bird flying in that place

I float a mere 10 centimeters from the ground

Crazy bird in a cage

Once as I was flying across the night sky

your arrow pierced my heart
Flutter-flutter-anxiety disorder, spasm disorder
That's how bird became a bird

In a blink of an eye
bird became bird

Knife-blade like chirps
Bird is definitely mad

Bird's shoestrings come untied, dragging on dirt
Bird's hair ribbon comes untied, winding a cypress tree

But I love, love flying
I love going far away

I write,
Angel whose tongue got bit by the mother-tongue dictionary
is polite to the point that its mouth is burning

Crow's Eye View 31

Today, I'm wingless
—Yi Sang [Kim Haekyeong], "Wings"

In Kim Haekyeong's poem 13 children take off down the road
In Kim Hyesoon's poem 13 birds fly above the children's heads, up to the
　　sky
13 birds keep flying up till they can't be seen from below
For 8 days straight they fly without eating or sleeping
They're so high up that they're flying across the black sky
The 1st bird says, It's terrified
The 2nd bird asks, Am I dead?
The 3rd bird says, I'm pooping diarrhea
The 4th bird sobs then falls from the sky
The 5th bird's supersonic prayer dribbles like vomit from its beak
The 6th bird chirps, I'm an arrow, then
thinks of how to commit suicide
I want to keep writing ruthlessly about all 13 birds
but that wouldn't be polite, for they've been endlessly patient
and it wouldn't be polite to Kim Haekyeong either who wrote the same
　　line—"it's terrified"—13 times because things were intolerable for
　　him, then turned the paper over
and jotted down the complete opposite—"don't take off"—so I decide to
　　stop

Really, the birds might not be terrified at all
Perhaps the 2nd bird is terrified of the 1st bird and
the 3rd bird is terrified of the 2nd and so on
This is how one nation might end up becoming a terrified nation
Terrified or not, birds fly because they can

Go a bit further and there's our country, the Republic of Korea
Doors of the nests along the pristine ocean shore
are left ajar like vowels
Welcome! Rooms wearing white aprons await
So birds keep flying

12 birds arrive on the west coast of Korea
In front, a vast reclaimed land for farming
Skinny, scruffy birds perch on the observation post like bowling pins
Birds haven't slept or eaten for 9 days straight
Birds are so starved that even the blood in their veins has dried up
In front, there is no sea

Crimson-colored hands of the mirage snatch up the birds

The 1st bird bashes its head into the asphalt
The 2nd bird bashes its head into the asphalt
Out of politeness, I'll stop repeating

Birds are falling inside my face, then the landscape, too

Inside-Bird and Outside-Bird

A frigid sound of a violin
Bird sweeps across the frozen river
and watches us from above
as if looking at the fish trapped beneath the ice

Bird crashes into the window
triggering a symptom

My nosebleed drips into milk
In the scattered crowd at the snow-covered square

two people walk side by side
It's cold isn't it?
No!
Perhaps we are the violin's cradle
The opening and closing

of the gap between you and me
as if it were alive
a lumpy, transparent bird
too precious to be touched

It hurts to look down from above
Two people walk side by side
like the way the light switches for the dining room and kitchen sink are
            perfectly in line

like two words that appear on the back of the page
written by my teacher, drowsy from a painkiller

How wonderful if there were no doors in this or that world

I finally feel it
that the world becomes as flat as a mirror if bird doesn't fly
that's why my bird flies even in sleep

Bird pecks on the glass again
triggering a symptom

From up in the air I can see
you and me walking
as if I were looking at the fish
trapped beneath the ice

Birds' Funeral

I'm at a funeral listening to the eulogy
I look out the window
Once I was sitting by the window and overheard birds talking
I was as startled
as the birds called startlings
Birds chatter:
How come I'm the only one with a room this high up?
What floor are you on?
I'm on the 13th
Really? I'm in the basement
This whole conversation shocked me so much that I turned into a bird
Dear Readers, do you have any idea what that felt like for yours truly?
I thought I was fluttering my wings—
the sensation of my wings detached from my body
Dear Readers, can you guess what that felt like?
Or that feeling of only the body plopping down on the ground?
Where's the birds' basement?

The eulogy is a report on cliché language
I do my best to listen intently
She says:
I'm so touched!
I think to myself, where exactly? Heart? Lungs? Or ribs?
I despise that expression—I'm so touched!
I try to think of something else,
about oystercatchers that dive one hundred meters deep
I pick at my ears because I can't hear the eulogy can't   hear
I imitate the eulogist
When I go down one more step d d deeper
her lips look like beaks pecking on feed
I end up saying to her, Shht shht shht
All the guests at the funeral turn their heads in my direction
The eulogist looks like a bird pecking on a poet's corpse
She thinks that she's exuding praise, so she keeps at it ardently

In my house, there's a bird on each plate on the dining table
There are knives beside the plates
It appears that we all have different memories of the deceased's bird face
Each bird on the plate is different
Why is she trembling so much? I pass a note to a poet next to me
He whispers, That bitch always trembles,
showing bird meat stuck between his teeth
Tok tok tok, the sound of the deceased's coffin splitting
swarms in and out of my ears like flocks of birds
And I say, Here, but here, there, here
But why does my voice swirl in one spot like water in a well?
Why do I talk like the eulogist?
The almost half-split birds lift their heads from the gaps in the funeral
          program
At times, bird with a human face
kicks up dust between page 4 and 6
Waiters wearing bird masks pour wine
Blood flows inside my head—shht shht shht

I want to sit under the chair
but the eulogy is still going on
My unfortunate childhood says, Shht shht shht
The author's unique shht shht shht turns hardship into something positive

Blood gurgles in my throat—shht shht shht
Blood boils like a broken TV—shht shht shht

Lately I can't sleep. I can only snooze with my head turned sideways like a bird's. I don't eat. The names of dishes disappear in my head. Perhaps it's because I'm too busy jotting down the voices of the birds soaring everywhere. Birds like giggling. They call their mates as they giggle. Birds remain monogamous even if five thousand of them take flight all at once. Birds can't help expressing love to their mates even if they're among the five thousand chatterers. Fever goes up as if I were a bird. I go to the emergency room. I go again the next day. Birds feed on my Ringer's solution. Birds steal my food. They even snort the fluid in which my memory is preserved.

I once read about an experiment that involved putting eye blinders on bats
The bats could still fly and catch insects as if they had no blinders on
Next, their eyes were cut out with scissors
The bats were thrown into a tunnel
They still flew with the same speed and precision
I asked the bats with bloody scabs over their eyes,
What are your eyes for?

Inside me birds dive into the deep sea, then as they resurface
birds exhale loudly
It's not even summer, yet I hear the deafening sound of next summer's
        cicadas
The sound of birds' wings beating as they flock to feed on the cicadas
I fall into the sea made of insects' wings and chirp,
How? How's taat taat taat?
Then the nightjar on my left that I can boil to extract oil from warbles,
Why let let let let?
The more I chatter the further apart nightjar's chair and mine become
as far apart as between Seoul and Moscow
My soul thinks, Now it's time for me to spread my wings and go home
When my soul and the oystercatchers surface from the deep sea all at once,
        they also suffer from decompression sickness
I want to go home   now

Birds' funeral is in progress
Birds carry dead birds on top of their heads, from bird to bird
up to the dark sky
up to the already prepared birds' graves

I look around—a flock of birds has filled the large funeral hall
I cry and run out in the middle of my eulogy

I can't remember where I left my wings

I can't breathe unless I'm up in the air

Korean Zen

Even if I don't blink
my eyelashes write on my face
(but I don't have any eyelashes)

I tolerate time
as I lift up strands of hair from the crown of my head
to write on empty space
(but my head's shaved)

For how long can humans endure silence?

But I'm listening to the typewriter
of the girl above my pelvis who is typing

(For how long can humans stay inside a poem?)

Bird floats me high up then
takes off alone

I can't tolerate the sky
like the way I can't tolerate poetry

I think of a plump girl called Ego
Tonight I need to starve her to death

Maybe I'm killing the future before the past
by killing the girl in order to attain nirvana

But who's breaking the swishing
windshield wipers of my heart?

I pick up the receiver of a red phone
that's been ringing nonstop
inside a pocket made of bone

It's that girl

Double Dog-Eared Page

Mommy, don't read this page
I dog-eared it, so you'd know to skip it

Birds shed tears, hammering the sky with their sharp beaks

I'm typing
a command:
Make the bird fess up!
Even if you have to hit it!

But what I really typed was birbirbirbirbirbirbirbirbirbirbirbird
faster than my pulse

Bird's wet toes
caress my face
Lipless, tongueless
bird pleads,
Please help me!

In this elevator, there's no button for going up
and the morgue is underwater

When I hit you in the kitchen
it was as if I was hitting a bird,
says Mommy

After I hit you
you went into your room
and quietly stretched out your wings

You
poor thing

(A silent night lit red with all the traffic lights of the world
I follow Mommy
I open the door deep underwater
That silent place where Mommy nurses an infant—that rock-a-bye place)

As if its neck is forced to hold up someone else's head

you

bird
little bird

nod nod

Regarding Bird's Respiratory Illness

Egg white seeps from the boiling egg
then disperses, spreading its white wings
Bird flies into the boiling water

The furry hands of atrophied wings
brush down my backbone
and unhook my bra
It feels so creepy that I want to cry

White sheet flutters like an egret with its feet tied
then like a jammed projector eternally stuck on the same scene
the screening begins
Every hole of my body is on view

Aborted infant living inside a hole has black eyebrows
then its wings grow
Bird flies into the packed soil

Mommy stares at the dead infant
hiding its big toes and mouth

Like the wailing ambulance, one dead bird
wiggles out from between Mommy's lips
With her scream
Mommy yanks its wings sticky with saliva

Even if no one is looking at me
my face keeps making a cruel face
Water boils inside me
and the birds flying inside the boiling water soar out from my face

(A tiny bird trapped beneath ice
endures a blizzard boiling up from below
I wanted to cup the bird in my hands
and keep it in my heart but
its wings never let go of the ice)

There is a custom of boiling birds in order to extract their fat

My arms sway like wings in the boiling water

Bird, Scared-Stiff

Strike bird's head with a golf club

Bird dragged out of its bed flies off
Bird with its hair tied back flies off
Drops its baby-hand-like claws—only its torso takes off
Just flutters away cluelessly
Feathers scruffy by the time it lands

The sky is already clogged with a green netting
When light is lit deep inside the mountain
it looks like the inside of my wide-open mouth
under a dental lamp
And inside my mouth a golf club strikes birds' heads
Birds fly off as if they've been thrown

Birds that live outside the netting
have insomnia
Every night, they quietly watch this scene
They watch with their bloodshot eyes

In the basement
a deaf girl curled up weeps

Birds fly away like bait on fishing hooks
The fishing boat is packed with fishermen

The doorbell rings scared-stiff
The golf club pushes its head in before the human head
Sorrow's neck snaps off

Tyrannus Melancholicus

Cyclone speaks

A small eyebrow floats away in the night sky

In my heart, the same eyebrow floats away

Like a corpse eaten up by maggots in just a day
the whispwhispwhispering
never stops—
Is it the sound of water inside me?
or the water rotting outside?

Full moon crawls into the toilet

Droplets of water from the leaky faucet
fill the bathtub and slap
water's buttocks

Water rots inside the living

I thought I threw a bowl of rice onto the floor
and rice splattered all over
but it was actually hatchlings

I swore that I would never call birds but

Mommy and I start like this
It's Mommy's turn
Mommy throws down the dinner tray

My heart goes whispwhispwhisp crazy
Cigarette ash fills my mouth

I don't raise birds, for
I rear water inside and out

Black lightning slaps the hatchlings' buns

I want to put socks on their matchstick legs
before someone snips them off with scissors

You trees, slouched like prisoners
Today's weather is famished
Soon it's going to slam down on you,
I warn the trees

A male student in my class walks by grind-d-d-ing his teeth

I could be mistaken, but I thought the chicks' black tongues had moved
        simultaneously

Somehow I thought of telling the little chicks,
If you want to become friendly with men, just let them touch you

Dwarf birds enter all the holes of my body and turn on the faucets
so I always wake up between 1 and 2 in the morning
My moist eyelids smell of ghosts
The endless kiss of my grandmother's black lips—she only lives in my
        dreams
No, no! My lips become wet
The chairs in my office are swept into the water
At the scary riverside
clutching onto the four walls my books get totally soaked

Birds bathe inside me
Birds can wash my insides meticulously like the way
they wash themselves with dewdrops shed by magnolia blossoms

The approaching cyclone says

Does sorrow also exist outside my body?
It's not sorrow, it's spasm
It's dark matter cloning itself
It's skinny vertigo
I want to shout,
The melancholic still has rights!

The giant bird that has covered my country stands up
Like I said before, this is all because I've called the birds
Bird paddles away by itself

Bird oscillates in unison with the fierce rainstorm. When bird takes flight, its wings can cover my whole country. It's nothing, nothing, I think to myself. My toes are so ticklish. Bird usually appears late summer to early autumn. Once in a blue moon, bird launches its raid at the wrong season.

Cyclone speaks again

Don't shake the beaker in front of mother and daughter
Don't drink the fishy pink grapefruit juice before bed

Mommy's well is deadly
The contaminated water is contagious
Broken Mommy, too broken to break anymore, says,
If I'm a nuisance to you
I don't know what trouble I'll cause next
I say,
Mommy, I will break first
What's the best reply for Mommy who says the same thing a thousand
        times?

Dear Saint of Suffering, dear Mommy who's heavier than the dark sky,

Please stop acting as if you're a white color, innocent and clueless
I always have trouble memorizing the chant after birds appear

As the ocean's surface heats up, water evaporates and rises from convection, then condenses. The latent heat flows like blood over the sky, warming the surrounding vapors. At this point, a severe low-pressure system is created by the strong ascending air. This is a proof that birds are forming. Before reaching this state, atmospheric pressure has already infiltrated my heart, zigzagging through my thoughts and feelings. Rolling its feet, singing, screaming, slithering through like a snake, jumping like a deer. Like a dormant sorrow, it raises its front legs ready to attack. Like the uncontrollable cosmic madness one woman faces.

Cylone forms
Cylone explodes

Cut the nerve fibers of the frontal lobe
Bird's five fingers fall off, plop plop
onto my cheeks

Cyclone says

It's so easy to slap and shatter the cheeks of a jar!
Why do I get bigger as I shatter?
Why am I the infinite field of black minerals?

The sweat-soaked bed is the birthplace of energetic birds. As birds fly from south to north, riding the westerly wind along the coastline, they switch direction, forming a big arc, and launch a raid. Birds swoop in at the speed of avian influenza. I'm just one bird, swarming with five thousand birds from head to toe. I'm five thousand shadows. I'm bird—there are only birds between the gaps, between birds. At times I'm alive, at times I drop dead. I clap five thousand times. I adjust my pillow, hoping to escape the claps. This time, the arc of birds bends in the direction of the clock, occupying my body in a U shape. The flock is sack-shaped. Enormous.

My arms float
My flailing legs also float
Garbage along the alley starts to float but the house stays put
House squeaks as it tilts
Twister hovers, sweeping up more garbage

My face is not smiling but my lungs are—laughing feebly
So what I'm a laughingstock?

My body is floating in water, yet my drowned lungs giggle
So what I'm really funny?

The funniest thing in the world—my mommy
The most incredible thing in the world—my daddy

Day and night, day and night, then night comes even when it's day
The melancholic loves taking a stroll
Oh ho! Oh ho! Magically, the melancholic enjoys heading out
to the black wings of Sea of Okhotsk
It enjoys riding the sneering

I'm riding in a taxi and ivy pelts the road due to a rainstorm
I roll down the window and wail, Mommy, mommy!

Every bird of the flock is as big as I am
then grows gi-gi-gigantic
This isn't bird, but my fluttering obituary, my elegy

Next, the ocean floats up to the sky

Cyclone howls

Why am I the only one floating?

I unfold all the letters I've received from Mommy-Daddy
The letters always begin like this,
To my most beloved daughter in the whole wide world
Every letter whispers
I shouldn't cry
If I cry they'll tear
When I gather all the letters, it's a black suitcase
When the suitcase opens, a flock of birds soars out

Every bird shouts,
To my most beloved daughter in the whole wide world

Mommy's given name opens my door without knocking
For the first time in my life
I enunciate her name
as if I'm calling my own child
Hey,
Soon.
Ja.
Then I add,
Do.
Not.
Open.
The.
Door.

Close up, I see birds moving like water inside me, flowing against gravity
Every bird is deformed

splashing like buckets of water spilt in the air
It's all because I've called out birds
Close up, I see birds scorched by electrical currents
I thought birds were water, but they were a luminous body
Each bird's scream is as loud as a cargo ship's
Sounds inside a human heart are even louder

My eyes and bird's once met. The world was never so quiet. Bird's eyes were like the eyes of a child quietly shitting blood. At the center of the vortex, bird's eyes were bluer than the blue sky. Bird's wings usually bend at 30–33 degrees latitude. A gigantic bird. A midnight orchestra. After landing in Korea, it's expected to make its way out to the east sea.

I'll say it again. The woman who's wearing the skirt as big as the shadow of my entire country is me. I'm so enormous that I can send a letter from one end of my insides to the other. My skirt is all water. It's so heavy that I can't stand up. All the silvery train tracks of Korea are on top of my drenched skirt.

I'm on the train, crying out from every compartment, Sorry, sorry!

I SHARPEN THE FOREST AND WRITE A LETTER

Mailbox

Should I say that I blush as I wait? Say or not that I'm waiting to be parted? Who first created the word pure?—naming something that doesn't exist. I send back whatever I receive like a woman sitting at a counter—what do I call someone like me?

Say that I bleed once? That my face is smeared in blood? That I'm a poor heart promptly sending out what comes in? A pale palm enters and exits my chest. Why does a primate's hand feel like it's coated in plastic? Is life a clear veil? I tell you bluntly, I won't keep you.

Yell inside the incubator, Turn on the light? Say that it's an overnight delivery? I wrap up an infant, write the address, and lick its eyes to seal them. I plaster it with stamps and mail it. Should I put a notice on the door that I'm open from 9 to 5 in order to send back the infants that keep arriving?

Say that I'm standing on the road with my chest open in a snowstorm? Should I attach the label Handle With Care and beg for my story to be delivered?

C Is for Conceal

I decided to spend a night at a house next to the cemetery wall
If I were to fly out the window of the house, I would immediately crash
        land onto the cemetery
The cemetery is the final refuge for those who lived nearby, but is also a
        path for leisurely walks
The neighbors strolled and tended to the cemetery as if it was their own
        yard
I had one foot in the cemetery and the other in my room
and fell into a state of rest and stroll, dinner and stroll, sleep and stroll
In my sleep the cemetery stood up like a giant and called my name
I think it was telling me to walk briskly
Naturally, shrubs and birds were dangling from the cemetery's gigantic
        body
Even tombstones were hanging from it
One day the cemetery called out to me as it was watering itself with a
        watering can
which then put me in a mixed state of dream and stroll as I got soaked in
        rain
Sometimes, I read the epitaphs while I walked
One day the giant announced while I was half sleeping and half strolling
that I should call out the names engraved on the headstones one by one
So I strolled while calling out the names as I would from my class roster
and soon enough I was able to call out every name even after I returned to
        my room
Sleep well~ ~ my potato~ my adorable potato~ ~ ~
Regardless of whether I was singing a lullaby to a basket of potatoes I
        planted
once a day or not, it was as if I was nurturing the death of the dead
like the way my potatoes were spewing poisonous shoots
Then one day I decided to leave the house and
that's because I was just walking around outside the cemetery
not eating or sleeping, calling out the names on the roster of daily sabbath

almost blue

Brass-winged-instrument sobs
flowing in the river it has made

It grows whiplike trees along the riverbank
makes the wind weep

makes knife blades float in the river
makes women gathered at a jazz club bow their heads
and stare into the deep-blue river

The golden, brilliant brass-winged-instrument submerged in the river

My lips crack and bleed
I gush out
till my white undergarments are drenched in blood
I can't endure myself

It feels like all the women in the crosswalk are leaning sideways

Dark mirror is drenched blue
Woman sitting in front of me is also drenched blue

Brass-winged-instrument howls
flowing as it makes the color blue

It climbs up to the blue corner and shouts,
Keep calm
You're doing good
Keep your eyes open and don't take them off your opponent
But why are the coaches all men?
My bandaged hands are tucked inside gloves
my long hair in headgear
my loose teeth in a mouthguard

I'm not hurting
But the boxing begins
Our heads tilt back, our breasts burst, yet painlessly
because we're submerged in blue

One person per minute
a soul lights the blue room of newborns
One per minute
a name is called out and you enter the blue morgue to identify the dead
Nothing hurts anymore

Lips rupture, then
teeth spill out
A mouthful of thumbtacks, yet bird bites down on the trumpet's
            mouthpiece

Golden pipe speeds
Windless but wind's bloodstain

The audience outside the ring stomp their feet, clapping
The howling sound system
Blue light streams down on my head in front of the mic
as if I'm the only one standing submerged in the river

No white towel yet

Again, I Need to Ask Poor Yi Sang

Dear colleagues of surkoreanpoemaordojunta,

I'm someone who raises stairs
I water them

My stairs grow tall like a melody
Melancholic step 5
Regrettable step 6
Sorrowful step 7

I go upstairs like the way my tears flow upstream inside me
I go downstairs as if I'm burying my sadness underground

My sibling stairs have lost their daddy

When I open the drawers of the stairs, Daddy's eyes flash open

If my painful knees don't exist, then stairs don't either

What if there aren't any stairs that risk the horizon?

When I lie on my side and hug my knees
the stairs inside me reverse direction

I go upstairs and look down with crow's eyes
I go downstairs and stare at the tail end of the numbers even further from
        year one hundredthousandmilliontrillion away

You can call me a conductor of stairs
You can call me an excavator of stairs

When tears well up
my stairs stack up one by one
When my sadness gets buried
the pitch-dark basement inside me expands infinitely

To prevent my stairs from spilling out
I circle the staircase from top to bottom and bottom to top

My stairs' lips and your stairs' lips meet and moan moan moan

Stairs didn't create my music
instead it's my music that has created stairs

However lonely house
     lonely stairs
     lonely bed
     lonely patient
     lonely coughs, ascending stairs

This morning you, my fellows of poemaordojunta keep ringing the doorbell
Stairs howl neck to neck

What I listen to, hiding inside the piano:
Crazy bastard's nonsense, what bullshit, kill him!
Why bother creating such a thing? Cut her piano strings!
What is this? This isn't music!

But surely you won't ignore the fact that
there's music inside your body that's far more complex than you

I don't wish to be loved by you
What I've made is merely a pattern of despair

a spiral staircase that chases after me and conducts me

Therefore, after listening to you
I shut my mouth and kneel
take two steps then crouch once
prostrate and raise my right leg, then turn over to lie on my back
unlock the door with my bound toes

stick to moths
shove my head into a rice cooker
switch my body with the whale's
clang the gongs with my heels
punch the ocean with my fists

to the basement of a basement
to the root of a root

Stairs, bite the bullet and rage!
Stairs, bite the bullet and endure the void!

Dear members of the poemaordojunta standing outside the hallway,

I'll embrace your knife with my hands

Please just leave my stairs alone!

Portrait of Fear

Flower blossoming in her hair is scorching hot—Sister is
Leaves are scalding hot even at the slightest touch—Sister is

Metallic apple above her breasts is even hotter—Sister is
Two front teeth that bite into the apple are shockingly cold—Sister is

Frozen tongue, so her body feels like a fireball—Sister is
The command living inside her brain becomes increasingly severe—Sister
    says

that the photograph of her family on the wall is boiling
that the picture frame is as hot as the pot handle

that she needs an enema because hot sparrows are crawling out of her ears
when she sobs like a quivering aspen tree

that black threads of her sewn heart are coming apart
that her waking dream is licking the bed, wardrobe, dining table

that a piece of meat she began chewing a hundred years ago is still stuck
    inside her mouth
that all her house pets are constantly rotting inside her mouth

Root of the flower in her hair is combusting inside her body—Sister is
Heart is damp like her clasped hands—Sister is

Letters to Your Honorable Hospital CEO, Your Honorable President
    everyday—Sister writes
You have a child and husband, don't you? Let's switch, switch places!—
    Sister pleads

Filling Out Customs Forms on the Last Day of the Month

> *Have you traveled to the springs at the bottom of the ocean?*
> *Have you walked in its deepest parts?*
> —Job 38:16

It was late at night, but a girl who lives in the ocean came to fill out a
     customs form

The form must be shared by three parties

Postwoman said:
One sheet goes into the postal cabinet
Another to the girl from the ocean
Nowhere to mail the last one

Another girl came to fill out the customs form:
I want to dry my mommy's lips wet from the tears of four seasons
I want to hug her like a tongue

Postwoman said:
Pick three deep-sea creatures
that might explode at your touch
Then she paged through the dictionary of sea language to check whether
     the form could be mailed
She didn't send it to the girl's mommy

Girls continued to arrive to fill out the forms
At the bottom of the ocean
there are mountains taller than Mount Everest
schools in the valleys
and even cathedrals
but you can't climb up to the top of the ice,
said the girls

Soon, the girl with a cold stare came to fill out the form
She returned like an abandoned, clingy pet

Top of the ice cathedral is too cold
Bottom of the ice cathedral is too quiet
Night postwoman couldn't read the girl's frigid, mirror-like words on the
        form
but she put it in the cabinet
Nowhere to mail the two remaining sheets

On top of her towering desk that appeared like the faraway night sea
a paper glacier with layers of sediment loomed blue

Children of the South Pole came for the postwoman at all hours
so that whenever she breathed she broke out in goosebumps and sobbed
        uncontrollably

In the morning you might turn into a scrap of paper,
the postwoman said when her shift was over, hugging a girl's cold body
Shame and rage appeared to her in quick succession

When the post office was about to close
the girls came back to fill out the forms again
Postwoman slept in the same room with them

(Next day when I went to the post office
there was a sign on her desk:
Please go to the next desk for service
Her dictionary of sea language was left wide open)

Candle

When you say Joy to the World
it's like—Joy, my death has come

When you say *Our Joyful Days of Youth*
it's like—Joyful day he murdered me

When you preach the Gospel of Joy
it's like—Please spread the happy news of my death!

Is it because of double p? Pappa*oppa*happy are in cahoots
finally coming for me

Get out, get out, get out of my room!—
I know I should set myself on fire to kick you out

But I wept the most when high school girls
their arms locked marched and cried—
Get out, get out, get out of my room!

When someone sobbing gets in the face of
another sobber, igniting in tears

ghosts bore holes through your red sleeves
and scatter on the first day of snow

and stars stay inverted
till they're caressed

When you say Lord of Joy gives us bright light
it's like—my eyes glow as they sprout from my body's ashes

When you put out this light
it's like—all the birds of the world can't spread their wings

Monster

I have
two legs that can make the five thousand migratory birds
landing on a reservoir take flight again
I have
smelly holes that can make all the dogs of our country howl
in the middle of the night

On my face, I have two bellows with bleeding landscapes inside them

I have
breaths that can burn out like candles
exiting the cosmos one door at a time

A pigeon flies into my windshield
A big thud
yet the pigeon flies off

I unzip the long zipper that runs up my back and pull out the monster
It wiggles out
My car overflows

I hold on to the steering wheel with my zipper still undone

A child runs out to the main road
to catch a red balloon
and the child's mommy runs out to catch her child
and a white rat as big as a house bolts out of her mouth

and the white rat swells up, blooming translucent
and when the rat's gigantic pistil and stamen soar up to the sky
and when the rat becomes so huge that it reaches the edges of troposphere,
        stratosphere
the sound of mommy's wails

Earth is like a lone squealing rat

I have a virus that can bury alive a million pigs into one hole in the ground
I have ten fingers that can topple a thousand statues of Buddha's disciples
        into the hole
I have

Eyetooth

Train is crying inside my pocket

Silvery chain gets longer outside my pocket

Passengers tied up in chains—I bark *kung kung*

Cascades of mountains retreat

Minty smell inside my mouth—is it blood?

Me and the train, phone and the mountains, cascades and the wind—we
    need to get on top of the rhythm to survive

Train makes a caller-has-nothing-to-report call

It feels like an ivory tusk is piercing, soaring through my forehead

Silvery chain coils around my body

Suddenly I'm terrified of checkered patterns

Train speeds up as if it's about to push the woman over a cliff

speeding like a telephone

I'm afraid of phones

You're in critical condition, I'm told

I pick up the phone while trying to escape from it like a bird sleeping with
    one eye open

Train turns its head to the right

Rail tracks made of jointed bones are waiting

Train is crying inside my pocket

Little Poem

Once upon a time there lived a big story and a little story.

The little story was so little that it was as tiny as a dog the size of an ant, tiny enough to flee through its collar, and so little was the story that it also cooked, washed dishes, and lived on a chipped plate, and its house was so small that the toilet backed up and the glacier melted and the youthful you trapped inside the black-and-white photo for decades floated by—that's how little the little story was.

Because I keep getting smaller, the little story is small enough to be sucked into the broken movie projector.

My night is even smaller, even smaller than a black bean, too tiny for you to grab by the hand, so I go around spilling it every night.

When I look down at Seoul from Mount North, it looks as if something got spilled on the city, so the buildings swarm in to lick it—that's how frenzied it is.

The little story is so little that even though it thinks that it is speaking, it's the same as not speaking at all.

There's only the word clean but no kleen, keen, cleat, cleek, cloot, clat, clot, so I have no idea what I'm cleaning with the little story—only shhit shhit shhit.

I sprinkle salt on an icy metal sheet and in the morning when a wild boar comes to lick the salt, its tongue sticks to the metal instantly and beneath the mommy boar her two piglets keep suckling her teats—that's how far the story goes.

The little story is so little that it just keeps piling up like dust on the postwoman's desk, so if you want to read the story I mailed, you'll need a dictionary smaller than a speck of dust—that's how little it is.

You say that you can bash my story whenever you want because it's so little, that you'll write my story instead, that my story is like an animal too small to be seen, living stuck to your little eardrum, but my little story crosses many bridges inside your brain and takes the third road where the path splits into three, and it walks for a long time and sets up house on top of your seahorse and in every dream you scream—that's how little my story is.

More Tender Heart

Poets were asked to participate in a treasure hunt
so I rushed out to the field
but I couldn't tell whether the treasure was a soft rock or a hard cloud

Poets swarmed in from all over the world
and discarded their mother tongues and said,
Let's learn a language that's about to go extinct
and write to each other
to appear to be
fair—as if

I quickly hid our secret inside the full-length film
fearful that you might find out—as if

In the pitch-dark night I hung a white wrapping cloth
and projected the film on it mute
waiting for the scene in which the secret is hidden—as if

There's a mailbox in the movie
bound to secrets like a dead child that keeps turning up alive
How scary it must be for the child to keep returning

In the movie we embraced tightly for ten seconds
as if we could love
without our feet touching the ground
singing loudly as we turn around

A wound about to heal
opens like an eyelid

and a drop of blood quietly
soars in darkness—as if

I mean, where is the hidden treasure in this poetry festival?

Postwoman

There are so many names in the world
and more souls than names
I feel like crying

I keep silent streets in my drawer like rolls of Scotch tape

isareambe
inonatof
andwithonlytoo

Mail arrives like grammatical particles
and I send it out all day long

I'm a farewell specialist, hugging a green desk

I put my hand in my underwear and pull on a string
My blood vessel is like a piece of red twine
My body is filled with organs that fulfill their farewell duties by themselves

At the moment I'm alone after mailing the white of the white eye
battling dewdrops that wet my sleeves

When I leave the post office, I'm like unborn music
I'm nothing like the glasses the deceased are wearing

I'm the future of farewell

Snow flurries keep slicing white knuckles, leaving them on top of the
          mailbox

Postwoman's blood pressure and pulse are printing out nonstop on a roll of
          paper

She puts up a sign, Send Mail, as if it were a tombstone
and sits beneath it all day

Sorry, I'll leave work after I send everything away

Mommy's Expansion

She's a white rabbit buried in snow

White sheets white pillows nice nightie my mommy
White rabbit lying still under the snow with its paws crossed

Her ears that don't listen to anything have grown up
When I go near them, they become filthy clouds

Like falling snowflakes
like fog on the river
Mommy's a bunny that can't be held

Human vegetable—is this term meant to insult or praise plants?
Mommy walks the hospital hallway filled with the souls of human
            vegetables

Long, long ago there lived a genius girl
She grew old and turned into a white bunny in her bed

What's your name? I forgot, she can barely speak
She became disabled and snow-white, growing wider and wider

What will we become after we grow up fierce?
We pull out the whitest-white bunny from under the blanket and shake it

Pre-Ghost

What comes out of my eyes
besides my loving tears?

What do my pupils taste like?
Do souls taste like them?

Can I say the light beaming out of my eyes is light? Say the light belongs to my
body because it streams from me? Is the glitter in my eyes already a ghost?
What can I say about the look in Mommy's eyes when she opened the door—
Mommy who cried for three months and ten days after Daddy passed away.
What about the light in my daughter's eyes when she saw my face in color for
the first time after I'd been floating in dark water for 280 days?

Do we see the world through the soul's heels?
Do we dream standing up?

What's that light beaming
out of the eyes of my family
as we say to each other,
Let's eat before the food gets cold
and share the body of living things?

What's that light reflecting
from two sips of water
spilled on the ground?

The gaze of the stars
hovering outside my window—what are they like?

What do you call the sorrow
that keeps on staring even after it's dead?

I Don't Want to Live Inside This Novel

Every strand of my hair hurts like a knife blade
as if my flesh is cut by the slightest breeze

Dwarf soldiers spill from the cracks in the brick wall
They suck all the energy
from my body

The night I read this novel and went inside it
a mutt's slimy spit landed on my cheek

Tonight's moon is dead
The sky is also dead

Dead birds' transparent bones fell
on the ground, slanted sideways like dirty rain

I said,
There's a saying that humans are no better than animals
so that's why you discriminate against animals

We've barely made it out of the country where terrible things
moremoremore terrible things keep happening
a country where a fiction factory is built inside a prison
a country where ghosts face each other like unborn twins

but you just cut out my story and paste it onto a piece of paper
Oh my god, I've become as thin as the paper

Trees become as skinny as pencil drawings

My dolls catch tuberculosis
My life gets invented

Now it's become difficult for me to say sky-blue sky, wind-blew wind

Will I be able to exit from everything on this paper?
If it weren't for this novel, I could keep on crying

I could jump over these dolls

As in the drawings of Henri Michaux
I want to become someone who exits my own text, standing up
I want to become the multitude that exits my multiple texts, standing up

someone who exits crooked letters, standing up
someone who exits cricket letters, standing up

I tread the whole page crookedcricket

But I'm inside this noisy novel, as noisy as the shack next to the railroad

This tearjerker is saturated with filthy saliva
a fake treasure map smeared by an old stain

dark moss in a pigless pigsty
even more worthless than the butts squatting around the bathtub
a stinky drool

Please get me out of this novel!

Pointed Handwriting

I poured the goldfish into a puddle from the fishbowl I was holding

I looked around to see if I could throw out anything else
Throw away my cat?
No, I shouldn't throw out any living things from my house

There's a dense forest in the middle of my house
When I lift up a piece of cloth
each tree gives off the smell of its genitals

The day my child didn't come home, I went into the forest

I went into the music hall to listen to the symphony, but even before the
orchestra began playing, a Steinway piano hopped around the stage like
a three-legged horse. The wind instruments stuck out their beaks like
flamingos; it's pointless to say anything about the cellos. I yelled out, Pull that
child out from the frozen puddle! My throat kept screaming and my heart was
like a pitch-black forest. The graves inside the forest hit me. They slapped my
face. The immense forest with its genitals exposed hit me.

I released a lizard

I released it daily, it slapped me, I paid it tribute
The lizard prostrated next to a puddle like a stinky rock
I released my beloved friends, teachers, and family
Then I didn't look back

Someone asked me, Are you calling farewell a forest?
When rain falls like a long, long letter inside my room
sad things happen and a forest begins to form, I answered

I knew that the more I told the truth the more sentimental things would
    become
The day I aborted my baby it felt as if I had swallowed a flamingo as tiny as
    a fingernail

The tiny flamingo danced up and down, and the forest grew bigger
When I fell asleep, the heartless feet of rats, lizards, and cats
crawled out of the forest and passed over my face
My dead relatives from the forest didn't want to miss the chance of seeing
    me defenseless
They showed up outside the window whenever I undressed

One afternoon of mine—I wondered if I was finally let out of the low forest

Inside my pitch-dark house I sense the enormous white forest
I feel the breaths of the souls of those buried alive with the dead

My skinny handwriting hiding inside the paper multiplies
like a barely visible sign, like a tiny insect wiggling its whole life

Forest, my forestbird, my forestSufism, my forestdeity
I'm all alone now—I'll end it by pouring myself out
Oh, how sentimental!

Right now, I'm writing in forest
I sharpen the forest and write

COMMUNITY OF PARTING

The Body of Parting

Daddy, why are your lips pale?
Why are your eyes faint even when you're sitting right in front of me?
Why does it seem like you're moving further away even when you're sitting
        at the dining table?

That time when our eternity began
That time when there was only the beginning
Daddy, you, me, and my siblings—we had indistinct wings
(In other words, we were all inside a single soul)
We emitted light, yet we were shadowless
Without body heat
our eyes were entranced by the faintness
We were in such a state then

We didn't know it then, but we were like birds, each trapped inside a
        lightbulb
We didn't know it then, but we were each trapped inside a transparent skull

Daddy, tell me what you've seen
But, Daddy, you only ask,
Where am I?
I answer with my eyes closed,
You're in a sunless place that's filled with light!

Daddy, angels can't embrace each other

I keep answering,

There are blurry wings
tiny souls
that flutter their long eyelashes mysteriously
that are infinitely small
like banished light
like clear rice pouring down

(The unexpected exquisite feel of every tiny grain)

(Oh, the souls of every single grain!)

Measuring the weight of the cumulus cloud
Slicing the cumulus cloud with a knife
Daddy, a hand went past your lips, your heart
caressed your face, then vanished
Measuring the weight of the hand's touch
Slicing the hand's touch with a knife

Infinity is freezing
Eternity is terrifying

Hands interspersed between the echoes returning from space
Pointless hand gestures—trying to cut out the faint voices

We begin our beginning
We didn't know yet that it was already our parting

Daddy, that place that took you away
One life enters the oblivious eternity that has just folded its wings
then it enters the transparent skull
Bird chirps inside the skull
the bird with feet cut off
doesn't know where to land

Our death had already begun
so we were all equal
Why didn't we know it then?

Daddy dressed in white robe, white head gear
about to be cremated
Daddy who betrayed me by dying
I'm going to betray my betrayer!

At that place there's no beginning, no ending
no already
no yet
no women or men

no Daddy or children
that's why everything's flat
that's why everything's infinite

I can't shake it off
Daddy, I feel as if I've already seen the future beyond your cremation
Dazed Daddy from the very beginning—it feels like I've seen you before
Daddy, you shouldn't have begun
Because of you there's time
there's parting

Daddy pretended to be my past but became my future
But now between us
wind blows, then suddenly stops
Daddy, it feels like the wind is whirling behind your back

The tree bends over as if guilty
White rats jump down from the branches
Daddy, it feels like the rats are gnawing, burrowing into you

New books stopped arriving
Daddy, like your bookstore that went under
Daddy, why do you keep your mouth shut?
Why do you hibernate while you eat?
It feels as if you're moving far away even though we're sitting across from
            each other
It feels as if I'm wearing a sock over my face

Daddy, I feel as if I'm standing naked
inside your shabby bookstore
bombarded by X-rays
a sunless place, yet filled with light
like in a dream
as if I'm entering the faintness

as if the angel stirring the cumulus cloud with its heels
is entering our mouths as we sit at the dining table

Daddy, I think our footless bird
has already discarded the morgue

That's why, Daddy, the dead me keeps greeting you

The me—splattered like mud
keeps extracting you—scattered like clear rice grains

Daddy, you pass by me swish swish
Daddy, the undertakers have tied you up like a sack of rice

You Can't Put Your Hands Inside This Box

A dark box
Remove all the six sides, yet it's still a dark box

You can't put your hands inside the box

Wish it were a snake instead
Wish it were a toilet instead

It can't be Mommy's naked body
It can't be mother and daughter on antidepressants

As long as it's not my family
As long as it's not our genitals, breasts, lips, eyes, anuses

All of you who are beneath my fingers

As long as it's not a poisonous insect, roach, worm
As long as it's not Daddy
Daddy's face is powdered for the first time in his life because he's dead
Daddy now has the hairdo he hates the most
Daddy still breathes after he's become warm ash
I carry the box of ashes
We ride together in a black limousine for the first time
I'm pregnant with ashes

But my hand goes into the box
(Mommy said, Don't put your hand into your hole!)
pushing its way inside
(Mommy said, Something terrible will happen if you do!)
into the air raid shelter
(Mommy said, Keep your bodily holes clean!)
into my sibling's tiny exploding mouth inside the shelter
(I'll smash your hands!)

into the bird's dense forest where the souls of our family members are kept
my fingernail goes in like a dog chasing a chick

Bird's genitals
Bird's anus
Bird's eyeballs
Birdbreast

Red blood vessels on birdbreast as if scratched in red ink
My sibling smaller than a fingernail plays a drum smaller than a fingernail
        toingtoing tapping birdbreast
My grandmother's skeleton has turned to dust, her soul wrinkled, tenderly

Like the way lower jaw comes out of a purse
like the way upper jaw comes out of a rib cage
rows of grandfathers are sitting at a park
with their birds out of the cages
The souls with severed wings are napping on grandfathers' laps
Maybe one of them is Daddy—I grope the birds to look for him

in line line line line line line line line line line
in line line line line line line line line line line

I fumble through the boxes lined up on the paved road

It's not the kind of box that makes my hands stiff
not the kind of box that makes my fingernails bleed
only my fingers giving off the scent of blood
Inside Mommy's womb five siblings tightly embrace
Her womb smells faintly of blood like onion peels

Creepy! Creepy!
When I put my hands inside, thin faces keep peeling off

Like seals and sea lions drenched in sorrow
my bare body is nameless

But we all have the same last name—Death

The shapes that are modeled after Mommy and Daddy

With a rolling pin and knife
press
slice
my heart and flesh!

My hand goes into a box filled with crazy birds
Can't breathe!—so my hand
is stripped?—my hand!

Help me, help me!
Please get me out of here!
Deep into my throat, my wound

Into bird's sour beaks smirking laughing in sleep
(My dirty octave that endures my crying shot up to the tip
of the lightening rod had to be rushed to the emergency room)

Mommy says, Please close the hole
And I say, Please put your face away

Fly, Hospital!

When I close my eyes and float up
I feel as if I'm drifting inside someone who's under anesthesia

Moon is shining like the lens of the patient's eyeball
and I'm sitting on the white of his eye
examining his sadness

We're experiencing turbulence, please fasten your seatbelts
Is everyone listening or sleeping?

In yesterday's news somebody opened the window and cut the rope
of a window cleaner hanging from a high-rise building
His wife wailed all night long

As on a plane there are first, second, third-class zones in hospitals and
        funeral parlors

Patients endure, strapped to the bed, in one, two, or six-bed zones

Everything in front of me is like the seawater
surrounding the weeping capsized boat on the TV screen

But daddies sick in bed
call out, Mommy, mommy!
What can their mothers in graves possibly do for them?
Their mothers are also looking for their mommies

Two eyes scared or scary looking
are stuck to the frozen window like double lightbulbs
Hospital flies far away at night
circling the Earth like a Ferris wheel

The inside is life and the outside is death
Life is a sealed bag

I think that the guardrail bed
is flying away

Down below fishing boats sail out from the harbor
and the big wildfire begins to spread

Rats multiply endlessly
like the headwaters of a river

Lapdogs yelp from the delivery van
flying across my dark eyes

As on a plane, there are first-class, second-class, third-class coffins at the
        mortuary
Hospital rows, squeaking across the sky-pond at night
pretending it can't hear me at all
even when I tell it to be quiet

Mommy, Please help me, help me, Mommy!
Dead Daddy, it's your nightmare

Birds migrating over the Himalayas
cover their ears

Winter Solstice Recipe

It's snowing
The creek
in the middle of the snowfield
flows like a spine

I make red bean porridge
The dark-red cough in my right lung
flutters like phlegm cake

On my way here
I sent out the invitations
without any names on them
I thought they'd all come

When I shuffled through
the white sheet from above
Daddy, you were standing there

When the red beans are done
I clear Daddy from my eyes
and add sugar

It's snowing harder
I can see the bird with a flowing spine made of water
stand and shake its huge wings
Tiny fish fall
like snow flurries

The falling fish are
silver-teaspoon-fish

1. Days yet to come
2. Please don't come, go back

All the sounds vanish from the landscape

What should I write on a Post-it
Daddy, goodbye?
Daddy, don't go?
I write down the winter solstice recipe

I knead white circles
and keep shoving O O O into the hot porridge
as if I'm shoving myself in
I think to myself, What am I going to do with dead Daddy all night long?

I want to touch his flesh
but it's a landscape of water and bones

I feel sorry for the days
yet to be born
I throw out the red porridge
onto the snowfield one ladleful at a time

Blood blooms inside snow

Bird Sickness

Daddy, I wish I could look at myself from above the way you do
I wish I were that bird drawing on the curtain
so I could easily perch on top of a pole
When the curtain steps out onto the balcony, I kick it aside
and fly off somewhere far

There's only darkness even when I open my eyes. My future is in front of my eyes—how do I look when my eyes touch the darkness? The prescription for when my sorrow is bigger than my body. I try out the manual of "Becoming Bird." I hang Do Not Disturb on my door. Total darkness. Silence. It's written in the manual that individual response times may vary, but that I'll reach a moment when I'll no longer be aware of the passing of time. My hands and feet turn cold, my face damp, and suddenly a blot on the ceiling appears in the shape of a bird. Hazy phosphorescent light like a lamp, emitting dreams. Spottedbird pops out like a hiccup. Spottedbird is hot. Spottedbird weeps. Spottedbird eats spottedants. Spottedbird catches spottedcrickets. Spottedbird feeds on spottedsnakes. One positive thing about being caught by spottedbird is that I tune out from tiresome warnings. I also tune out from the comfort of the endless chirping of birds perched on power lines. My toes turn as cold as metal skewers while I incubate the spottedbird. My eardrums become so thin that I can hear the maggots three miles away. I coddle the lukewarm spottedbird that's not tears or blood. Then silence and I whisper together. I can hear, but I can no longer speak. My throat only makes screechy screams. It's written in the manual that when this happens, I'm almost at the end. There's food left for me outside my door. As soon as I smell the scented candle, thoughts fall out of my body. As if the spell cast on my body is broken, all the thoughts I had during my lifetime become a single lump. Memory falls out from my body. It's a lot smaller than I'd imagined. The phosphorescent light keeps welling up from my body. My body in which the phosphorescence plays is as cold as the North Pole where auroras play. I fall into a stupor. Cold oblivion and hot oblivion occasionally lift up my body. Just then, someone opened the door and peered in, but I was barely recognizable because my face had changed so much. They say it was like opening the door to a filthy place, as if a ghost were manifesting itself inside. I persist with my beaming phosphorescence and my thinnest eardrums. I listen to the moonlight caressing the stained glass of a distant church. No suffering. In case, Daddy, if our eyes happen to meet, Daddy, you won't know what I'm looking at. Because I was on edge all night, birds flew out from every hole of my body. As if the ceiling made of black paper was peeling off page by page. Soon it's chilly as if a hundred birds are staring at me. Even in total darkness, I now gaze into the distance. Then a flock of birds, each bird takes a turn, pecking at me, peck eat, peck eat, peck, peck, peck, peck, peck, peck, peck, peck, peck, peck, peck, peck, peck, peck, peck, peck, peck.

The smell of cooked yolk, a metallic-fishy smell. Bird's temperature is minus 42 degrees Celsius. My armpits are on top of emptiness and silence.

I just keep going somewhere faraway

Like the heart that jumped out alone from its body
I'm bird in critical condition

Now that I've become bird, birds seem so wretched
I want to nestle under their warm breasts every minute

Flying crows are featherless, they're naked pink
Thunder is also pink

Is There White Light for Us?

Bundle of rags under the dining table

Wings are bunched up
as if gasping

I want to be cool like the cold birds of the winter sky

But my hands tremble, for I despise my family so much
Every time I breathe, rags heave up and down

Flickering sound
Crashing sound
Apologetic houses everywhere

I keep having dreams about a bird under my older brother's heel

Over there, tiny Mommy is under someone's heel, but I can't go and rescue
        her

Girl wraps the rags with her clothes and coddles them
That girl can't be me

In the morning I brush my teeth hard, but they don't turn white

I wonder whether my bones are white even if I don't brush them

White Vindu Chakra from Daddy
Red Vindu Chakra from Mommy
Raw meat dyes my teeth daily
I steal a candle from a temple
I think about lighting up white my apologetic house
Smell of the Tibetan temple I've visited
Smell of shiny floors like all the faces at the temple
Smell of flesh stuck to bones

I think I've reached the top, dragging up my wings
but when I turn around there is no mountain
Ah, the dreadful white mountain is gone
Color white's dormant period is brief
I write a letter from the flattened mountain,
You're going to become filthy for sure
Damn mountain! How dare you perform the color white?

You died far faraway and returned
Daddy, like an owl,
you perch on the dining table
and see night during the day
night during the night

Daddy, when you're too embarrassed
you swear every other word
like I swear at myself in the third person

Everybody says it's my fault
and not my brother's fault

Daddy, your flesh-colored head
spews white hair like a white trumpet

Older brother's flesh-colored head
spews black hair like a black trumpet

Sin redder than blood becomes whiter than snow
Jesus the master washer is on Mommy's lap, giving a sermon
Jesus, Mommy's Jesus, you raise up so many lilies
Jesus, you are lilyphyxiating Mommy!

Bundle of rags under the table
Girl spews rags like a rag trumpet

My body has no color white
I don't perform color white

P— P—

I'll call that place of mine Ay-yah-fyah-lah-YOH-kuul

The shape of Daddy's and my guilty conscience
My synchronicity and nonsynchronicity
begin p— p—

Nobody has given this a name, so the birds that don't know the name
(We receive bird's name when we are born
but we don't receive one at death)
fly high into the night sky

I lie down in the injection room to get a shot every week
and stare at the same stain on the ceiling

The stain that Daddy stared at from his sickbed for two years

I want to shout, Leave my Ay-yah-fyah-lah-YOH-kuul alone!

My p— and Daddy's p—
The moment our p—'s vomit blood through the hole
the moment birds flying in the night sky peek out of the stain
When I wear my watch
the whole world also wears a watch for five minutes
then I deliberately get on the watch-train
Watch-train scatters in every direction

My vibrant hair loosens itself on the two rails for five minutes straight

Icelandic glacier comes into my embrace

whimpering
p—
p—
then blue blood like god's
buried deep in the ground
suddenly gushes out
shooting nine meters high—
that place

is at that place

Bird shitting in flight
crashes into the window of the hospital room

White-colored-noise Ay-yah-fyah-lah-YOH-kuul dissipates quickly around
        the world

Like a trembling cold wrist, birds of dawn fly over the roofs of all the
        hospitals of the world

Brightly lit glass elevators
shoot up to the sky through the rain-soaked forest

The more I go down below the higher the elevator rises

Then momentarily in Iceland, like a blue wound—Ay-yah-fyah-lah-YOH-
    kuul

Bird's Diary

Daddy, I become bird in the room where you died
My ribs become round
I become bird always on the lookout

The room with shrunken landscapes neatly stacked on a bookshelf

A Mayan woman crushes a dead man's skull
and bakes the head with only its skin left in the hot sand
The shrunken head smaller than a fist
is excavated from the sand
It's the face of a bird with long hair stuck to it
She threads his ears and wears the head around her neck

I burrow a hole in the door and peer at last night's bird

The whites of the bird's eyes have vanished
only the black pupils are left

I lie down at the bottom of the swimming pool and think:
There's a bird in my room
a bird that can give birth to featherless chicks
As I think this, a gigantic bird suddenly soars up from the bottom of the
    pool

I hold on to someone's waist on a motorcycle
speeding at dawn and think: I have a bird
As I think this, a huge bird is on the backseat of the motorcycle

I have a shrunken face like the skull's skin hanging from the Mayan
            woman's neck
I have a bird that becomes more bird the more I'm alone

Bird that runs and bangs its head against a wall
What's going on?
Bird never stops
running back and forth

with its pointed beaks
stuck to the bookshelf
like the spectators' heads moving
side-to-side nonstop during a tennis match

There's a bird in my room
There's dizziness of a thermostat stuck in my hot armpit
Are you alright? I ask
Bird bobs its head, always social
even if it's all alone
Even though I've become hypersensitive
I keep returning to the room to check on the bird
worried that it might fly away

I become bird moremore
I become glimpsebird, suddenbird, briefbird

I become bird on a jam-packed subway train
I become bird with a brain a thousand times smaller than mine
I become trembling bird
between teeth-grinding shoes swarming
onto the train's floor like a pack of rats

A mister sneezes inside the elevator
I become bird

A pigeon gets run over by a car under the electric pole
I become bird

I become frequentbird, morefrequentbird, moremorefrequentbird

Sleepless bird
like a bird hatched under the midnight sun

Bird that stops singing when I peer in
It sings only after I depart

Bird that vomits
an enormous forest from its straw-like throat

I take off flesh first
next skeleton
Bird that has nothing left
but bird

Bird
watches shabby me staring at it

Now I can't turn back
The one miracle in my life
made me like this

When I peer into the room again
bird speaks to me for the first time,

Go!
Go!

Daddy, in the room where you died
I become bird

Shredded Bird

Clear skies all over Korea, aren't you scared? the weather comes and asks
      me

As soon as I imagine a bird falling through the vast, deep, blue sky the weather returns and asks, Dark clouds all over Korea, aren't you scared?

At the psychiatric clinic of Professor H, I pretend that I'm not staring at the rows of patients and their guardians sitting on the sofa. Everyday I'm scared of wholenation, wholecitizens, wholeweather, wholenews.

When I unbutton my pajamas
scaryscarybirds fly high
from my scaryscarybed

I shred my poetry books daily and fold birds
I fly "Bloom, Pig!" up in the air

Birds go where they can't be seen and die alone
My books also go where they can't be seen and die
They've taken a beating before they croaked

Every night I see the same face
when I lift the funeral hemp cloth to pay my condolences

Poetry-or-bird or bird-or-me or wants-to-say-it's-me-bird or this poem
wraps itself in gooseflesh beneath the feathers

Today, a Pineapple Express over the wholenation, aren't you scared? the
          weather asked again tirelessly
I answer without imagining anything,
I'm scared of Pineapple Express

While I walk in wholenation rain, unable to open my eyes
a foot bigger than my cradle steps in

Daddy, I'll cut your toenails for you

Thunder and lightning keep asking, Aren't you scared? Aren't you scared?

Today I become exactly five thousand birds and
fly into the downpour of toenails
I storm off, flying high up
Every bird has a different weather system, different mental illness

Today's five thousand weather forecasts, five thousand horoscopes
Aren't you scared of today's wholenation depression? the weather returned
    and asked

When I look down, wholenation is teeming with hospital wards
In one of the wards, I answer, I'm scared of the Express

Don't Fly in This Country

Daddy, I was born here, yet I'm told to escape
I've lived here all my life, but I'm not allowed anymore
This nation is out looking for me
Borders are sealed
I'm told to get out
All of its territory rejects my footprint
They all know my face
They'll kill me if I breathe
I'm not allowed to cry

Daddy, I escape into the water
My body floats when I close my eyes
Nothing but water

Daddy, Look! I get even thirstier under water, that's why my body floats up
Look, I can even lie down on walls
I can also walk on ceilings
I roll up my body and fly
Books fall from my shelves
My dishes fly away
My house leans sideways

Time drags its feet slowly along where water pressure is high
A thousand-year-old turtle crawls out from under my bed

Here, bird walks with its ten fingers over its face
worried that someone might recognize it and point a finger at it
worried that its body might float ridiculously in front of people

Daddy, When I lower my head and quietly fly down to the bottom of the
      building
my teacher sitting at the bottom of the ocean says,
It's so difficult to die
Go up toward the light, go higher
Push up your butt!

Sun sits on top of sleep like a yellow houseboat
and a lonely diver's tears well up from his chest

You are bound to lose your shoes in water
You are bound to lose your cell phone

You are bound to lose your passport

Right now, I'm ill up in the air
I'm deathly ill, unbearably thirsty
I want to open my eyes
but my nation says, Wait till I catch you!
All of its territory rejects my feet

Bird Shaman

When bird arrives
I'm like a distant punching bag, trembling in fog
You all have lovers in your embrace
but I've bird in mine
Those with birds can recognize others with birds
We greet each other
Amongst us, as birds
we point to a certain dance and say, That dance is
birdless

I'm clutched by bird
the way the veins of leaves clasp the green color

Ten fingers over its eyes, bird is soaking wet

I've let go of someone

When I arrived on the island, I kept having dreams about birds
Birds hanged by the neck with legs drooping down

One day I stared at the birds and
it seemed as if they had something to tell me
The old woman who owned the inn replied in the island's dialect
when I told her about my dreams
I played the recording of the old woman to a student working
at a coffee shop
Many people hung themselves on the mountain
Old woman's daddy and mommy hung themselves too,
explained the student,
She doesn't want to be buried
on the mountain after she dies

Uniforms by day
Bayonets at night

ordered the ghosts to stand in line
and told them to slap each other's cheeks
Ghost Son was told to slap his Ghost Daddy
if he didn't, he'd get stabbed
Hit me! Harder! Ghost Daddy shouted
at his Ghost Son,
said the student who worked at the coffee shop

I paced back and forth like the punching bag in fog
thinking about bird of a different era
what spectacle it might have seen

Birds stretch and contract their wings
I wondered,
Who tied the birds up
by their feet on the tree?

Then I became curious
When the eyes of bird and human meet
who gets to be the soul of all creation?

When I land on an unknown planet where only birds live—
how should I ask them?
What memories do you treasure from your time here?

bird bird
bird bird
bird bird
bird bird
bird bird
bird bird

Bird wailed like the shattering mountain

Trembling like a punching bag in fog

someone who had let go of someone
said to another who also had to let go,

Bird,
Birdie, please tell me what you've seen

Isn't That Photo Black and White?

Shave the head of the runaway moon
tie its ankles, put it in a birdcage
then feed it and nurture it daily
After the moon is all grown
unwind its body
so it can weave a shroud for me,
said Daddy

When I sit in front of the window and press my hands against the glass
my hands are higher than the distant mountaintop
I can grab the entire mountain in one hand and caress its thighs
I'm much bigger than the landscape, which never takes its eyes off me

When I press my nostrils with both thumbs and
spread my eight fingers like a bird's crest
I become a huge bird, taller than the tallest mountain in Seoul

I stand next to the window and play the game of getting bigger all day long

Moreover, I play the game, so I can compete one-on-one with Seoul's
     landscape

Now it's the hour of red dusk that pokes my nose
Envious of me for staying by the window, the sun gives off a scent of yellow
     pickled sea urchin as it departs

By then the curtain in my room is outside the cloud
It's very far away
When I close the curtain, dark clouds come in

My hand towel is hanging from the mountaintop
It's very far away
Every day I go to that distant place
to wash my face as I dripdrip water
Sometimes I go naked, dragdrag
my squeaky slippers, carrying the wet towel

Umbrellas grow on the faraway field
A friendly daddy and his polite daughter pick two umbrellas
and paint rain as they walk—how beautiful!
My daddy said,
Everything looks lovely from a distance
I want to keep Daddy distant like my wet towel
Daddy and I have only talked twice at the dining table in my whole life
I'll reveal what we said later

I repeat,
I'm bigger than the landscape, and I live in such an enormous house
that to fall asleep I have to row a boat to go fetch my pillow

My house is so tall that sometimes I have to catch a bird for a pillow

My house is so remote that
sometimes I can only fall asleep when I suckle, dangling from air

And how about this?
In my house, sometimes I have to wear a veil and row a boat
to reach my bird perched on the knife-sharp horizon and feed it
then bring over the blanket still wet with blood
and cover myself with it—only then can I fall asleep

Nevertheless, I take a photo of my dead daddy
Daddy stops unwinding the moon's body and asks me
as if we were still inside the womb,

Isn't that photo black and white?

Adverbs, Fly

Daddy, you always wake up at that hour.
Not in my time zone, but in the dead's time zone, at that hour.

Daddy, a new daddy showed up
like the way you whisper inside my crying.

His close-cropped hair was as wintry as the dawn and
his butt cheeks were smaller than cherries, poking the well of my tears.

Is it Daddy? No, bird. Is it bird?
No, a face, like snow flurries, like white flour that I stir with my hand.
My face vanishes after bird lands on it and takes off.

Only the quiet echoes of adverbs or absence of adverbs
remain in the spot where my face was.

I'm whitish like life that disappears even before it has a name.
My head becomes empty like the North Pole made of paper.

I cover my eyes with my right arm and swoon
on Verona Cathedral's cold floor.
I thought it was that hour again.

Daddy, your time of death is 11.
Daddy, I had a premonition of your death at 4 in the morning.
I shouted, Daddy! out the window in my dream.
One bird flew by.
Bird's neck was creepy like the night bus driver's neck—somehow it was
        like yours, Daddy.

Everyone gathered at the cathedral lights a candle for each of the dead
and sings Assumption of Mary.
Today is National Liberation Day in Korea.

Like water leaking from the ceiling.
Cold birds
one by one.

Daddy, you're a tiny coat, the size of my palm.
You're wearing a little overcoat like the ones newborns are dressed in.

You endure the coldness of death
like a tiny, shrunken life.

Daddy, when your delirium begins the Korean War starts up again.
Daddy, you always crawl onto the battlefield carrying a shotgun.

The blanket falls down from your bed and, Daddy, your candle
keeps flickering in the trenches of whichever side.
Mommy's a nursing officer, and I'm a medic.
We charge toward the screaming soldier.

Mommy and I kept asking you,
Daddy, do you know who I am?
Daddy, do you know who I am?
Daddy who has forgotten nouns and verbs answered,
Already earlier already earlier,
shouting only the adverbs again,
already earlier already earlier.

I leave the cathedral and pull a suitcase as noisy as an ambulance with my left hand, then my right, back and forth. What's inside my bag? Are you in there, Daddy? Tiny Daddy wrapped in white paper, like a gift wrapped in North Pole.

Daddy, when the little overcoat that brings you wherever flutters
the rippling landscape that has lost its owner and its weight follows me.

After we are all dead
the world
left only with adverbs
enfolds me.

Between already and earlier.

Jellyfish Are Ninety Percent Water

Lately I write scary words and tie them around my neck
As I was walking slowly down the hall
a student asked me

Professor, why do you only write bird lately?

I went to the underworld to invent bird

Little umbrellas stayed stuck between my toes
like jellyfish drifting in the ocean currents

Daddy in white—I bound his hands and feet together
First I tied the rope around his hands, strung it around his toes
and tied up his feet
so he'd fit into the narrow casket

As soon as Daddy put on the new hat that looked like two hands
somewhere in my body I felt a frail bird's feather

The letters that dying Daddy didn't finish
were left strewn on the blanket

I thought about bird flying freely in the ruins
bird that will fall if I don't keep writing

The paper on which the magic pathway to death is written
gets pressed down under my pencil tip

Lately I wear the letter written by the dead around my neck

Bird will take flight
after I pluck all the feathers from my neck and finish writing

As an eagle can stretch the moment of
catching its prey to the moment of carrying it off
the dead can look back at the hour of their death
slowly, very slowly all day long

I put three coins in his mouth and said

Daddy, please use them for when you fly away

(In Korean, you can't call your daddy in the second person)

(You can call professors in the second person only under the blanket)

Like the elevator door that stays open
only when you keep pushing the button

like pressing down on the piano pedal nonstop
so the transparent bird won't fall from the sky

like the umbrellas of jellyfish
needing rain, so they don't turn into jelly

Daddy, you mustn't fall
I pluck feathers
jotting down what bird's saying
I keep writing

The next day, another student asked me

Professor, Professor, why do you always hide your neck?

WHY DO WOMEN THINK THAT ANIMALS CAN SPEAK?

Eternal Bathroom

There's an empty house
It's been vacant for a long time
I don't know how long

One TV monitor lives in the empty house
As you know, it has no audience

Its screen changes more slowly than one-three-hundred-sixty-fifth of a
        frame per year
Time passes more slowly than when a blind orangutan's eyes gaze at the
        black sun

In the bathroom there are stalls for ladies and gents
Girl enters slowly, much more slowly a ladies' stall
Boy enters slowly, much more slowly a gents' stall
Marble floors show through the cracks of closed doors

Cleaner than a clean city
Cleaner than a clean chimney
Rows of sinks and toilets cleaner than clean buildings
Children slowly file in

Fish scales bud one by one on their bodies from sadness

Their entire bodies are covered in scales and like the two fish are sadder
        than them

The children slide into the water

Inside the monitor smelling of disinfectant

girl's white shoes, white knots
boy's white cap, white socks

Because the screen changes so slowly
the way a river flows slowly in a dream
like wavering silk

like sad fish, wiping tears with the silk, flowing slowly

No one returns to the river regardless of how many years it has flowed
The empty house hasn't turned off the TV for decades or thousands of
        years
It stays on like a deacon at a church filled with infinite joy

Girl to the ladies' stall
Boy to the gents' stall

We're left only with memories that play back in black and white
Intensely cold memories
Ultimately, we're earth's trinkets

Ultimately, we'll end up facing each other with our eyes closed

Question: Can you see the children's faces?
Question: Did they grow up to be a lady and a gentleman?
Question: Where do they go every day?

They slowly disappear into the house, waving calmly, coldly
But the never-vanishing TV screen stays put

A horde of silent organisms with suckers on the eaves of the house
Insects lift their heels and crawl under the eaves slowly, very slowly
Someone was about to strike the golden cymbal of silence, but under the
        eaves

a set of eyes gazes endlessly into the mirror

White melody inside the white music pours

into my ears slowly, as slowly as the time it takes for an ant to drag a dead
        spider
over that hill and snowy mountain

Inside the slowness

girl enters the ladies' stall
boy enters the gents' stall

But that someone who never appears on the screen
Why is she combing her hair for so long in front of the mirror?

Vanished Mommy Vanished Kitchen

When I followed a vanished kitchen, I only got to meet vanished kitchens.
I found out where they all lived.
I even found out how they recognized one another.
In the morning, like us, they fetch milk, read news, drink coffee, their
        clothes brush past on the bus. But there is one thing.
A vanished kitchen doesn't know that it's a vanished kitchen.
It takes a leisurely stroll down a tree-shaded lane as if it were walking along
        an arcade.
Even though the trees are rootless, mountains are weightless as inside a
        mirror
a vanished kitchen goes around in a circle saying, Spring has come!
        Summer is passing!
clueless about the fact that a ruin is a ruin.
As I follow a vanished kitchen, wind hurts like a kitchen knife.
Quiet sunlight stings like blood on a chopping board.
Bitter smell of cooked dust in the frying pan.
Does a vanished kitchen know that it can never return even if it takes a
        single step from a vanished kitchen?
Terrifying things always happen to the poor, they come closer like the
        bloody head in the basket I've carried around my whole life.
Vanished mommies sit in a circle in a vanished kitchen and peel the head
        the way they peel an apple.
When you eat dinner in a vanished kitchen your spoon becomes smeared
        with blood.
Don't smell the vanished kitchen.
Don't open its window.
If you do, it'll do everything in its power to disappear.
A vanished kitchen also cooks the way the deceased love more intensely
        than when they were alive.
A vanished kitchen can disappear again
the way the deceased can perish once again.
As if submerged in a mirror's mercury, it shimmers like a missing person.
In a vanished kitchen, a thousand disappeared pigs,
ten thousand disappeared chickens,

a hundred thousand disappeared fish.

A million disappeared cries.

When I follow a vanished kitchen, it mashes the warm eyeballs, letting the
steam rise while it gives me instructions.

Don't wake the vanished kitchen ever again.

If you do, everything inside the vanished kitchen will open its eyes.

The world's vanished mommies will put on their aprons and hold up their
knives.

You must finish this poem in the kitchen, then turn around and go like the
blind with eyes open.

The Stretcher

The man carrying the stretcher isn't dangerous.

The stretcher is friendly. Carry the stretcher downstairs. When you hoist it up high, you bend down, and when you bend down, you raise your arms.

The stretcher shouts, Rescue! Stop the pain!

The stretcher can't release the hands that are holding it.

The stretcher can't take the elevator. Can't ride the bus. Can't ride the subway.

The back of the head in front of me looks familiar. It's the head that held up my face as we kissed. I peeked at it in the mirror. It's the head that held me when I fell, it caught my breath as I bounced up. Bodiless, I used to stare at it. But I mustn't look at its face. Don't look back! If you do, I'll die.

The stretcher is giggling because it's out of breath. Hurry, hurry! then it giggles.

I repeat, the stretcher is not dangerous.

I wish the stretcher would feed me, change my clothes, bathe me in the morning and get me out the door, carry my bag, even wipe my child's runny nose, but most of all, laugh and carry me around like this.

As soon as I think

the stretcher is running. I'm heavier than when I was alive. The soullessness is heavier. But as for me I'm light. I'm lighter than a chick just hatched. I'm so light that I can't make out my own body. I can go far and return in a flash.

At Byeokje Cremation someone in jeans, holding a small box, scatters white ashes by the front entrance, then leaves. A mound of flour-like ashes on the grass. The woman's crinkled photograph listens to the wind at the entrance. The fortune teller said to the woman, Only one person will be standing at your death bed. Even that person will abandon you.

The stretcher goes downstairs. The motion light on each floor turns on and off. The stretcher is lowered one floor at a time. I notice the ceiling for the first time. The patch where the paint is peeling off. A little bird peeks out from it. Bird's pitiful face. Bird's toes and chopsticks. Bird's eyelashes slathered with mascara. As I said before, the hands holding on to the stretcher are doing just fine.

I wish I could live on the stretcher. I'd sway like on a boat, but that's fine. I'd still do laundry, wash my face, and sing. I'd mumble like a fish that has secretly come up through a crack in the hull.

I'm actually a mermaid. I've come up from the deep sea, so my hair's cold. My lips are blue. I look as if I'm crying, but I'm not. I can't walk now. The fishing hook has poked through my vocal cords, so I'm voiceless. I'll end up thrown onto a mat. I'm more expensive after I'm dead.

Sylvia Plath has reached the bottom of the stairs in the stretcher. From now on she won't die anymore.

The stretcher is set on top of the wheels like luggage on an airport security belt.

The hands that have let go of the stretcher are frightening.

Empty hands are frightening.

Not

I don't walk without music
I don't wear a slip without lace

There's a drum that bleeds when you beat on it
It doesn't leave the dance hall despite the beating

Shattered sea with a shattered boat, shattered night
Shattered boat doesn't depart

You must dance, holding a candle in front of Holy Father
Candlelight reflected in the water doesn't wipe off the blood

Torment, rippling with torment, raises a pale bone at night
I don't look back even when a lifetime of my faces call me

I don't cry inside the water because it's echoless
I don't depart even if I'm not here

Not
yet

Abortion Boat

I've become sensitive to light
Every time light brushes against my bleeding lips, it gnaws on them

I draw the black curtain across my forehead and sit at the dining table
The light grabs and twirls the crown of my head like a police interrogator
My plump, tight fists get pinched by light
instead of me

My mood swings have gotten worse
I was determined to be unaffected by my mood swings
From love to hate to fear to fatigue
I developed an impulsive mood disorder

In Agnès Varda's *One Sings, the Other Doesn't*, women travel to the Nether-
lands for an abortion before it was legal in France. After the abortion, the
women go on a boat tour through the canals of Amsterdam, and so they call it
an "abortion boat." The scene of the woman singing made me feel as if I were
listening to the song of her meaningless, empty womb. Aborted infants are
cremated and the women embark.

I dribble in the middle of a sentence
A long mucous drip
even though I'm not crying

Perhaps I've lived too long with drawn curtains
Suddenly, a tree climbs up to my head like a buck
even though I'm female
An infant heart grows on the tree
It ripens
I throw down my fork and knife and run out

As I run, the tunnel runs beside me like a dog
The tunnel cries and follows me, becoming very long
The woman who just had an abortion but still has a baby runs

When she exits the tunnel, her baby comes out
but when she enters the tunnel her baby sticks to her again

Rebecca Gomperts' ship leaves the Netherlands for international waters with nurses and doctors and pregnant women from countries where abortion is illegal. When the ship anchors briefly at the harbor of a country where abortion is banned, the Virgin Mary on board is the first to disembark, holding a plaque, "My womb is mine." Then burly men surround the ship, shaking their fists, Leave! Leave! The women's Netherlands rides the wave.

I've become sensitive to light
When I'm scratched by light, my skin bleeds like when it gets scratched on
        cement
On the spring branches blossoms of dribbling baby hearts

Red-Bean Handstand

Whenever Jung-yeob wants to leave home, she does the dishes, wearing a
      backpack
She even tosses her bag down into the garden from the second floor

But above all, she pours her energy into drawing a single red bean
First, she puts the bean on a train or big boat

Then beans begin to spill out of her pocket uncontrollably
Beans instead of fingers when she takes off her gloves
Endless beans
Between thighs, between toes
beans can't hold back like tears, like menstrual blood

A mound of beans in front
Beans between teeth
Beans until the bean moon rises

Whenever Jung-yeob wants to leave home
she stares at the sky through her crotch
A plane in the bloodied sky

Jung-yeob is the night of a crimson downpour
She adores roads flooded with red waves

The Seoul Arts Center shoves its head into the sea of beans
like the Boeing 746 swallowed by a typhoon
When the soprano hangs upside down from her seat, shakes her hair
and sings Madam Butterfly's "One Fine Day"

the gigantic woman's gigantic baby
opens its rice-seed-like eyes and
dangles from mommy's womb
giggling out loud

A deep place
not this place
when the bloodshot moon between thighs
caresses all the world's followers of beans
between every praying hands
beans

When a mommy delivers
at the end her placenta
spews energetically
Bean! to the toilet of air

Jung-yeob's menses hangs down from air
Jung-yeob's two nipples dangle beneath them

We dangle from air too, wearing out our shoes
Beneath the pilot, passengers, and hair flows equally
the sea of
beans

The immense sea and the sound of beans being washed in an immense bowl

A lone bean's melancholy sliding down her neck
Loneliness swallows a bean while sucking on it
Honestly, a single bean contains every emotion

This can be said to be a story about a drop of blood forming outside her
        body

Jung-yeob ties the laces of her running shoes
as when she was still single, in the front lines as an undercover labor
        organizer
fighting tooth and nail
against the world

One bean
a rootless bean
perhaps a lone fear

First, I drew it, a single red bean,
Jung-yeob tells me,
One red bean instead of tears!
I put it on a plane
then I drag the plane down the hallway, past the bus stop

Bean!

Face That Refuses Anesthesia

A smooth stone appears as soon as the river dries up
A drop of rain falls from the clear sky
and the stone encounters one more torment after having endured countless
        ones

Face is warm even after all her hair has fallen out
Face is so hard that needles can't poke her

Face dazed after being slapped, clutched by my right hand
Face carried the rocks from the demolished sidewalks and unloaded them
Why did I leave that woman here?

The fallen rocks nearby had the woman's
fine blood vessels, red cracks on them
How could she have slept all these years stretched out at the bottom of the
        river?
One day when I sped far away by train
scattering my flesh all over the tracks
a bare face spilled out as the door of the gas chamber opened

Face accepts the cloud's murky shadow
pushes her moist heart down under the rocks
turns around in the hallway, goes past emergency and intensive care to
        somewhere far, far away

leaving not a single weeping hole by her bedside

It pulses

A Blizzard Warning

When I open your letter, the boxes with birds stacked neatly inside open

The flock of birds from your letter mashes my trees, my dense forest
Birds pluck off and eat all my early-sprouted sore nipples
I've become the whitest ruined field

You say that you feel relieved after your confession
that our screen has dissipated
that you're wrong, were always wrong
You say while clapping
that you've healed
that you're saved now
with the smile of a dead garden on your face
and that, moreover, you understand me

Your confession destroys me. It destroys my mommy. It destroys my sister. In
the dead garden a parade of whitest birds. The past that you can't tell anyone
about—do you really want to know? Want to hear about it? Bird threatens me,
slaps me with its wings, then takes off its wings and pulls down its underwear.

All the ~ 爪 word endings that have left before me are falling
They fall down like trousers, holding hands, in pairs, running through the
        blizzard 爪爪 爪爪 爪爪

Part ~ed
Di ~ed
Forgott ~ed

Your same dreadful confession once again
(also known as) my past, suffocating the sprouts
You're not here, only I'm here ~ed ~ed ~ed
You dress my naked body in a shroud all night long
You bury my fingers and toes in the snow
You tell me to feel hurt

You tell me to become a wreck
become a poor, lonely woman

You say, What if we bathe each other in the blizzard for the last time?

You sing and clap, O Pure you! Clapping like a mongrel puppy. Why? Why?
You say it's all my fault since I asked. You say it's an unspeakable secret, that
you'll keep it forever, then white birds everywhere, I die, then the footprints
of a snowman like an avalanche that comes looking for me in the middle of
the night.

Shitty word endings that make my past!

Chorus

Boys sing, standing
They sing in unison
The guy with the clearest voice is motherless—even his father has run off
The guy singing in the lowest key is an arsonist—he grins while lighting a
      match compulsively
He's drenched with joy in a big wildfire
That tone-deaf guy, over 70 years old, kidnapped a girl and hid her in an
      attic
He tied up her feet with a huge chain lock
The guy finished his military training long ago, yet it's never been erased
      from his body
The girl killed by the bass singer still hasn't been found
He's cutting up the dead girl

One guy's victim—the skeleton has turned to dust under the rock. Another
guy's victim—the flesh has peeled off and is now a house for fish. There's
also a victim nobody looks for. Boys are singing. Undercooked sausage, tripe,
fermenting radish kimchi—are singing.

On a slippery steel board, the corpse is singing
With black butterflies tied around their necks boys are singing

Men who've won the warmth and love of women!
Let's sing "Ode to Joy" together!

Good, very good! I follow the guy
Good, very good! I kneel at the guy's feet
I'm a guide dog, and the guy's like a blind piano tuner
I've never once answered him, but
at the end of the silence a storage unit awaits
filled with broken pianos
He makes me kneel between them, but
even before the guy raises the conductor's baton
I speak like a broken piano

I take my pants off, but

Like soldiers carrying rifles with bayonets
the prisoners recite the poem written the night before
The drill sergeant is a former poet
In the yard where there are hardly any former poets
he likes memorizing the poems he's written outside prison
He's always a former poet
Tears spurt out like piss—poem
Beats his wife, then embraces—poem
His wife's hair flows down like rain—poem
Male lyric caresses—poem
He wants to cry every night, but he shits on—poem
(Any poem that enrages him because he can't understand it must be destroyed
He has a poem about wanting to hit a woman poet he met at an awards ceremony)

Girls sing, standing
The girl with the clearest voice is a mommy slapped by her son
Givemegiveme don'thavedon'thave—a battered mommy
The girl who sings the highest has sinned the most
She cuts her hair compulsively
She cuts her forearms
Outside she's solemn, but
when she comes home she locks her door
and washes off the shit she's covered in
She keeps many secrets, separate, in her heart and body
The woman, the main alto, is a housekeeper—she lies naked on a sofa,
        eating sweet buns filled with red beans while her employer is on
        vacation
The lyric of this chorus is so childish that I want to cry

However, we already know about these disappeared women. Their names
are already posted on a website that pays tribute to them.

Girls are singing. Difficult-breathing, pulses-racing, sweating, palpitating, face-turning-pale, darkening-complexion, gasping—are singing. It's like a song for those entering a gas chamber, a furnace. If you can't sing the happy song happily, then you must die.

They sing like the corpses lying on the slippery steel boards
White dress, white shoes, white veil
A wedding dress or a shroud? It's confusing what's she's wearing, but she
       hits the highest note

Joy! Joy! Joy! Beautiful spark of gods!
Daughters of Elysium! Drunk with fire, let's enter the light-filled sanctum!

I Want to Marry My Grandma

I didn't have to shut Grandma's eyes so tight.

I plant a seed in each seam of Grandma's hemp-shroud skirt.
The seeds sprout inside the seams.

Grandma always said, Don't become a cabbage-liar.
I tend the talking cabbage patch.

Someone who sends sweet sticky rain and
someone who gets happily drenched in it meet.

They say they are crazy in love. They want to marry. Each in a white dress
for both wedding and funeral, they want to marry. Millions of water flowers
bloom in heaven and earth.

Rain washes Grandma's legs. Her body extends from the mountain north of
Seoul to the toll gate in the south. I sit on top of Grandma's forehead and
write a line starting with "I remember Grandma" a hundred times.

I think of an umbrella that can cover Grandma's entire body.
I think of an umbrella that can cover me and the wedding guests.

Grandma, now you have a lot of land. This is all yours.
Grandma, when you were alive, you only had one dress to your name.

Soon the cabbages that were dangling from the dark sky
begin to break open above ground. Sticky cabbage heads.

The children in the cathedral's dark confessional room press their palms
          together with fingers pointing up like sunflower seeds.
They pray so the dead can never live again.

In rain, I think about Grandma whose eyes I'd shut.
I think of Grandma and me getting married in rain.

H Is for Hideous

He raised a flower vase to be his wife

The vase was so quiet that he didn't dare ask her anything

He told her, Stay home
When I come home, raise the corners of your lips

He enjoyed hiding his body inside the mute vase
The vase stank

The meterman who entered the house said, I had a strange feeling
I felt as if thousands of eyes were secretly watching me
That feeling of being in an empty kitchen when a faucet suddenly turns on
       by itself and water gushes out

The vase never did a thing in the house
It only held a rotten flower in its mouth
It only rattled the windows, cabinets, and glasses all night long
Sometimes it jumped up on the table and bashed its own head into bits
It could only lay its body in a straight line at the same hour, same space, and
       fly fast
It could only float up from bed with its hair down for a few minutes

But when you stared into the husband's eyes for a long time
you saw a crazy, homeless, mute woman wiggling out

He had a reputation for avoiding eye contact, being shy

After he died, the first thing the vase did was wash her hair in the middle of
       the night
After he died, the second thing the vase did was stare at herself in the
       mirror for a long time

After he died, the vase screamed every morning as if her face were stabbed
      by a pick

At dawn she went up to the roof and beat on the washbowl as if sending a
      fire signal

The police officer who received a call about the noise asked,
How many years have you lived here?

I don't live here
I'm just housesitting
I change the water in the vase
I get mail
I clean the shadows
I give birth to babies,
the vase spoke for the first time

Owl

Can you see? The owl soaring? Sitting and shitting bean turds? Never blinking once? So exquisite that its creepy feathers stand up? In pitch-black night, like a metal pipe, lightning, gale, the dying bird strikes your retinas?

I only stare at the night.

Your freezing fingers that grabbed my hair. Your hand that felt like a baseball glove deep in my warm bosom. Your sharp pinkie fingernail that broke my yellow moon. Your dirty fingernail grown long for ripping open a pack of cigarettes and picking your nose. My glass wristwatch that cracked like your eyeballs. The back of my head that fell onto the corner of the bed but didn't feel like part of my body. The huge steel umbrella that opened out from the inside of my body. The eight sturdy ribs of the umbrella that I felt one by one. The sound of the siren of the ambulance that took someone else and not me.

Even during the day, I only stare at the night.

A woman who's lost in the woods meets a male owl.
The woman asks,
Do you know where my mommy went?
The owl answers,
How would I know your mommy? Why do women always lose their way in
        the woods? Why do women think that animals can speak?
The owl rips open the skin of her face and gnaws her eyeballs.
The eyeless woman becomes an owl.
She becomes a female owl perched on a female tree.

The bruise soars, the bump soars above the bruise, and above the bump one hundred black parasols with a thumb-sized feather attached to each soar one at a time. Dewdrops of sunlight slide down from the top of each black parasol and fall. Owl is an animal that never gets drenched in sun. Even in the light it can't see what's in front. Bird. All the open parasols on its body make the light slippery.

When I open the closet door, there is a big pond, and in the pond the big shadow of a tree, on top of the shadow, a warm rugby ball, a black pupil without the white. I bring my eye 1 centimeter in front of the pupil, yet it doesn't budge. It only keeps staring at itself.

Bragging About My Dress

I look for my dress as soon as I wake up in the morning
I feel relieved when I see it still hanging stiff on the hanger

The fact that a dress has no thoughts is a lie
The saying that when a dress cries three times the whole nation goes under
       is also a lie

I don't feel lonely because I have my dress
I get anxious about being lonely again without it

But I can say that my dress is a birdcage
When it's windy, it feels like I'm wearing an oversized birdcage

My cage flutters in the wind
It feels as if a pianist with a hundred fingers on each hand
is lightly lifting me up in the air

When the wings sprout from my hips
spreading till they're no longer visible

I feel as if I'm caressing the lightest thing in the world
Somehow I feel sad to float so high up

My eyesight becomes perfect like the horsemen of the plains
Giddy up! I can ride my dress and fly far away

My bones are hollow like a flute
so every one of them can sing and whistle

The night my dress embraces my breasts and weeps
The night I blame myself—it's because my dress was too revealing (was it my
       fault?)
The night I pillow my face on my knees wrapped in my dress

The saying that you must beat your dress every three days is a lie

The saying that the plates break when three dresses get together is a lie

But because I'm nothing without my dress
I worry, What if I don't come back as a dress in my next life?

The night I put on the darkness, my favorite black dress unfurls
This feeling of a black ribbon around my neck unwinding
and the lights on my dress twinkle like the nightscape of Seoul
This feeling of infinite wings slowly taking off
like an insane stingray roaming in the deep ocean
Next, this feeling of a gigantic sparkly dress silently floating away in the
      clear sky

I'll leave my dress behind when I die

Beneath the dark cover of the cart / splendid coffins made of ebony / are swiftly dragged by the strong mares / with shiny dark-blue hair

A barrel carrying five crying mommies rolls along

Their tears are cold and the sun is blazing hot

The sky is blinding, the air is warm, today's corpse hurries into the fire to be cremated, and a barrel carrying four mommies rolls along

The barrel with the four crying mommies keeps rolling along without stopping to look around for one missing mommy

The wheels turned by the crying make a racket as if glass cups piled high were crashing down all at once

Long strands of hair stick to a barrel, wiggling like moist snakes, laying eggs

A barrel with three endlessly crying mommies rolls along

From the distance the road looks soft as if covered by a row of mattresses, but close up it's full of pebbles and ellipses, and a barrel with two crying mommies rolls along the bumpy road

One day a mighty mare with shiny dark-blue hair suddenly jumps up and down like the blind reading a famous novel in braille, and a barrel with two crying mommies rolls along

A barrel with one crying mommy rolls along like the glass cabinet thrown down from a high balcony

The mare treads along the path, dripping with sweat

A barrel of tears rolls along in scorching sun

The children are still missing even though their mommies have all left

An empty barrel rolls away like an old piano full of hairline cracks

Autism, 1

I was playing with my eyeless pal monkfish in a plum orchard when some man carrying a net showed up and beat my monkfish. A bump swelled up on the crown of my head, and my forehead bled. And when I said, I did it because of monkfish, my monkfish said, You can live in the ocean then, and my classroom teacher said that I needed counseling, and the head teacher said that I needed to be hospitalized, and my PE teacher grabbed my hair. When my classroom teacher shoved a curtain rod into monkfish, my mouth began to bleed.

Monkfish is on my feet
Crows are on my shoulders
My baby is inside my fallopian tube

Mommy called firemen, fumigators, and even detectives to search every corner of the house for monkfish, but in the end she slapped my face. Professor Kim, I'm telling you this because you say that you can see my monkfish, but I know that my mommy is lying to me. The firemen and fumigators are all lying to me. The counselor told me to try petting and pinching my monkfish. At night monkfish lives inside the fridge. Whenever monkfish eats, I become bulimic. The kitchen floor is slippery with my vomit. When Mommy wakes up and hits monkfish, I cry. When the toilet overflows, monkfish also overflows, and my hair gets drenched. Mommy told me to leave home. Please get out and die!

Poor monkfish.

Monkfish enjoys shoving its body into its own big mouth and closing its lid
    with its own two hands.

I was sitting in the plum orchard with my monkfish. Unripened plums were sour and blue, and crows crowcrowcrowed, and Mister asked me why I was in the orchard, why I kept dribbling. I dribbled soursoursour even when I heard the word plum, and Mister threw my monkfish into his net. Mister took monkfish to his house and locked it up in a room.

I couldn't fall asleep because his bed was too dirty.

Autism, 1000

I'm someone who draws a sunset as lips
I'm someone who hangs teeth in the middle of the sunset
I'm someone who strokes the sunset as if it were beautiful beef
I'm someone who paints the sunset like a diseased mouth

The woman has a dress on
over her bloodied slip

We'll heal you
We'll comfort you
So confess!
So confess!

Filthy words from every direction

I'm someone who draws
monkfish teeth
on the Pope's face
more than three times a day
more than thirty times

Pope's hands are up on the dining table
Things dragged up from the deep sea, things that flew in the sky
things that used to run about in the meadows
trucks, carts, ships
all enter the hole dangling from the chin of his holy face
The holy consciousness of his mouth!

Pope's underlings in white outfits circle me and shout:

For one woman who writes poetry you need a thousand doctors

Teeth dangling from the top and bottom of my wound turn crimson

Speak!
Speak!

A thousand laborers on excavators are digging up my tongue
Infants with gaping mouths are endlessly excavated from my mouth
but I'll never confess

because my thighs bleed when you stab the confession I give birth to

When my gums take off their slips all at once and dribble
a thousand deep-sea monkfish unzip in unison and dribble

I'm a woman who pisses a toothed sunset under my skirt
After I finish pissing, I insert a full moon
between my thighs and coddle it

Straitjacket

On my first day of school the smell of my teacher's breath
On my wedding day the smell of the officiant's breath
The smell from writing that offends women

The same smell as this outfit

I've recorded my perpetual departures
but I always return to the inside of my outfit when captured

It's criminal to tie up a tornado
It's catastrophic to lock up a liquid that has reached the boiling point

I don't cry even when you label me as a rightist, leftist, modernist, pro-
        Japanese, and every name of illnesses
You can have my nose dribble and phlegm instead

How can you say to the fish that the fish net is its outfit?
How can you say to the fish that the fried outfit is its coat?
When I'm in this outfit I feel as if I'm inside a radio
It feels as if every citizen is paying attention to what I'm saying

I'll apologize since every citizen is waiting for my apology
I'll apologize for the rest of my life and from now on
everything that comes out of my mouth will be red apples

Why does apple (I) need to apologize to apple (you)?
Apple (you) and apple (I) are apologies (for what)?

The outfit with strapped hands and strapped sleeves

A single outfit

The smell of my heart stabbed by my hands automatically poised to pray
The smell of the ethnic minority woman's hand, divvying up a freshly
        caught pig with the group sitting in a circle

In the room light baptizes through a powerful lens
But no one can enter the room dressed

Even the birds must take off their feathers
The fish must take off their scales
Trees, too, naturally
In my room everything is nude

When my old leather gloves stretch toward me
a whiff of toilet
My outfit reeks of sweat

Hit me
Hit me
The bird has already flown away

What you have hit is
just a void wearing an outfit

It's bright inside my outfit!

Princess Naklang

Lightning strikes my brain. It reaches my chin. Next, it strikes all the way down to my left foot. A brief pause, then it strikes again. Humiliation with shock, fear. Soon the lightning strikes again. Piss stench as I go up the stairs. This is the end. I want to die when I'm out of here. The woman takes off her top and lies down. The nurse carries in a bamboo container that looks like binoculars in flames. She ties the container to my waist with a black strap. Then pulls down a tin pail hanging from the ceiling. A fat, tin anaconda opens its huge mouth above my belly. I look down at the woman from the clothes hanger. The woman is being roasted whole, naked.

I spot filthy dogs in wire cages carried off on bicycles. I spot them often.

Insane lightning. A harsh insult against a woman by a woman. This time it's very harsh. When her mind calms, it trembles from fear. Becomes insulted again. Tears well up. A traditional doctor bends the woman's head back and pokes her nostrils with acupuncture needles. Next, he instructs her to bend forward and let her blood drip. Blood spills into a tin lunchbox. He then pins a medicated needle next to her left eye. Before she can tell him that's the wrong side, he pins another needle. As soon as he pulls out the needle, she yells, Not this side, the other side! He replies, Ah, that side! Then he pins a needle next to the right eye. He pins a needle on her head. The woman has needles pinned all around her eyes. She might as well be wearing glasses studded with needles, a hat studded with needles, and as she drips tears and blood, she turns into a barbequed hedgehog with smoke coming out of its belly. She turns into a female animal under the hands of a police torturer. Every day she comes here and lies down on the narrow grill.

Beloved dogs from my childhood arrive. They take their turns arriving.

It's pouring rain inside me. Water drips down the stalactite cave inside my head. Blind lightning is coming. Definitely a lost lightning. Suicide lightning. Thunder's sibling. Pain's underling. A relative of Zeus. Bastard lightning. Radioactive lightning? Every time it strikes, I become deformed. I've three hands, then my head splits into two. I've one hundred feet that run nonstop.

My body's not running but I'm speeding. The people inside me keep still but I'm running. I'm them but they're not me. They shut the windows on me. Next, they beat me up. Chopsticks aim and poke the meat on the grill.

Dog crouches next to the dwarf's toy box. Dog barks.

I'm sitting in line in a classroom.
My newly washed face for receiving sorrow.
My swollen heart for receiving anxiety.
My busily shriveling limbs for receiving fear.
My perfectly combed hair for receiving despair.

Bathed dogs are sitting in line at an animal shelter.

A woman enters the hospital's desolate waiting room where MERS virus has raged. She's the only patient to arrive for her appointment this afternoon. Not a single person in the country trusts the hospital, yet she decided to trust it. I can't stop her. But I decide that if she gets infected, then I'll think of this nation as a disaster nation. The entire medical team comes to work wearing masks because of the woman's appointment. She takes turn lying down on all the sanitized beds. The medical staff are friendly. The electrical monitors above the bed get hooked up. She and the examining team are the only ones in this big examination room. They all have their masks on, but the woman takes hers off. The doctor electrocutes the woman's face with something like an ironing pad. Her pain appears in the light—zapzap. Even in here she's the only patient. She's moved to tears by their kindness. Today, in my eyes, the woman is a princess. She roams the hallways surrounded by her servants in white. In the big sparkling-clean washroom she encounters countless towels, soaps, and sanitizers. Princess rents the second floor of the hospital. The four checkout desks are there just for the princess. Those wearing masks are also there just for the princess, to calculate her bill and schedule her next appointment. It's so peaceful here. The contaminated emergency room is shut, but on the second floor the princess can go from room to room by herself. Princess is lying down with electrical needles pinned to her face.

Princess strokes my hand, It's alright, it's alright. The sparkling-clean alleys where MERS virus floats around are vacant just for Princess. After I leave, the hospital is closed down. Princess is trapped inside.

Stinky dog barks.
An echo slaps the cheek of Seoul's Mount North and comes back.
Every time it returns, a different dog arrives.
Fattens, getting dirtier and dirtier, so a shy dog arrives.
Every time the echo returns, a louder noise arrives.
Lightning-like, wild-dog-like dog.
Dog bites and doesn't let go.
Dog doesn't eat, sleep, gets grubbier by the day.
Dog becomes so big, as big as Mount North.
Shitty dog shits on Mount North and runs off.

Dog yells,
Princess, tear the skin!
Tear the drum!

Woman's Woman

Mommy, I'm here in a forest of fluttering eyelids

Birds and trees have different sexes but
all the trees in this forest are female

Mommy, why did I come here?
After I walk for a while, I come across a sign that says, "Think Again"
"Think of Your Mother at Home" is also written on the sign

Long ago when you held me after giving birth to me
a shadow was also born and was watching you

Mommy, there are several signposts around, "You Only Live Once"
Some trails are closed with signs, "Do Not Enter"

Mommy, why did I come here?
Women who departed, weeping inside me, gather in this forest
where dark sluggish trees lower their ankles
and roam the muddy ground
where the feet of birds flop down

Mommy, here the women I abandoned
have become all-female-family and all-female-race and
they wait, wait, wait
It's a gasping forest

Mommy, like I told you before
in Lima
I met the car I once sold
The same make, the same color, the same "Yield" sticker written in Korean
And you said, What's the fuss? There are so many cars like yours
Mommy, my car became a taxi
Looking much older and as if it had been waiting for me for a long time
it put on a sad smile

It was rumbling and blinking
happy that we could finally meet again
but I wasn't happy to see it at all

That woman came for a memorial service, then discarded the photo
That woman took off her shoes and closed the eyelids of every tree
She had three tattoos on her thighs, "I Will Never Forget!"

Was the forest waiting for me like the car I abandoned?

Mommy, to be honest, something chases me every day
puffing like an Adam's apple

Dark trees ask me, What took you so long?
as they swing their sluggish limbs and roam the forest

Mommy, who did I come to meet in the forest
with my eyes still open?

Hypnosis Woman

How do you feel? *Lonely. I feel as if I'm in lukewarm water. Feels like I've become massless, weightless. Feels good.* Please return to the past. What do you see? *Light. I can keep going inside it. The light surrounds me. It's so bright that I can't look at it anymore. Please put the sleep shades on my eyes. And feminine napkins below.*

You can see but you can't speak. I ask, and you answer. You can only live in the world of answers. You eat, but I tell you what you're tasting. These shoes are delicious! When you eat the shoes, you become vivacious. You want to eat them every second—my shoes. Even my toes.

Spit. Grab tight. Walk quickly down the hallway. Your heart beats hard when I get near you. Your heart aches when I'm far away. You smile when you see me. You don't smile at just anyone.

From now on, your body will lean to the left. You can't stretch your body to the right. Your bag is dragged along on your left side. The food on the tray spills to the left. You've got a ringing in your left ear. Your beautiful right side is mine.

When I say TV, the TV hypnotizes you. When I say sewing machine, the sewing machine hypnotizes you. When I say calendar, the days from 1 to 31 hypnotize you. When I say 1, you raise both hands. When I say 5, you take off your clothes. When I say 6, you open your legs. Now, the numbers are commands. You're not permitted to open your bag. My voice is inside your bag. Wipe your tears with your hand. You're surrounded by my replacements.

You can't interrupt my speech. You're a one-person space shuttle circling above the infinite orbit. You can only respond to me or NASA. You can't return without me now. At last, your heart's hypnotizing you, isn't it? Your heart only responds to me regardless of your own will. Try shouting after me: My heart is yours. *My heart is yours.*

Repeat!

I'm your goosebumps!
I'm your orgasm!
I'm your pocket!

You're tired now. Your legs are relaxed. Your eyelids keep drooping. Moonlight puts you to sleep. Are you asleep? Good. You'll forget about today. You'll wake up after the third knock. When you awake, you won't remember me. As you take off your shades, you might have an inkling of something.

—The night wind is quiet. The wind that doesn't carry a command is not a wind. Water tastes really great! Where did the person who told me this go? Without the commands I'm not me. Water tastes like water. Since no one tells me, Now you can take one small step and walk out, I'm not me. I'm nothing like the mirror on the wall. The voice that said, Climb, climb up the hypnosis, the voice that lived inside me, has vanished. I'm not real without the voice that took me to that place instantly. Without the No command I'm not even No.

Bird Rider: An Essay

Long ago, I read a story about a woman who turned into a cat. I wrote about the story in my notebook. When the woman's grandmother passed away, she complained of tummy aches, meowed, scratched the floor, scraped the dirt, acting just like a cat. Even when she was hospitalized, she undressed and hid under the bed, meowing and scratching anyone who came near. She made herself bleed by cutting her fingernails too short. She said to her mommy, "Let's die together!" It was impossible to communicate with her. She could only converse after a long treatment. She said that when she heard a cat's meow, her dead grandmother appeared. Her grandmother adored a cat they once had. But the rest of the family was mean to the cat, so it disappeared. Her family denied that the cat had ever lived in their house. Once she might have heard her grandmother meowing, chasing the mice away. Later when the woman was asked again how she felt about cats, she replied, "Cats are unpleasant animals." The woman was mentally ill with a very low intelligence. She couldn't differentiate the world of senses from the world of imagination. She allowed the mixing of the two worlds and believed the imaginary was the real. After the sensory experience, the imaginary followed, and they both manifested somatically. The woman ventriloquized the cat with her body. When she imagined that cat (grandmother) was entering her body or that her grandmother was calling her as if she were a cat, she went into a trance and lived like a cat. As I read the woman's story, I thought to myself, isn't this the same as when I write? When I write poetry, doesn't my intelligence also diminish? Don't I also have a mental breakdown, and doesn't my body transform into womananimal?[*] I realized that all these symptoms are reflected in the persona of my poetry.

Living trapped by viruses, surrounded by culturenature, and exposed to all kinds of media—writers, self-help books, chefs, singers, filmmakers, even comedians—I don't want to be comforted, yet they pounce on me, to comfort me, to empathize. Startled, I get frightened. And, conversely, I become even more frightened when I'm asked who my poetry comforts. Therefore, when someone even utters the word comfort, I want to run and

---

[*] I coined the term "womananimal" in my book of essays *I Do WomanAnimalAsia* (Munhakkwa jisŏng, 2019).

hide. I don't think I've ever comforted anyone with my writing. Moreover, I think literature betrays the readers' desire to be consoled. Perhaps literature crosses into a zone where consolation can't intervene, evaporating any possibility of comfort. Just as there is no geometric or genetic consolation, literary work merely constructs an afterimage or alternative symmetrical pattern of the event that occurs. The ventriloquist lives inside literature. Ventriloquy is a deception. The writer first deceives herself. And she deceives the reader. Both are aware of the deception. The persona crosses into a zone of literature, the symmetrical world of existence. Thus literature is a lie. Fiction set as reality is a lie; poetry set as language is a lie. The ventriloquy of literature moves, riding the spiral of lies. And so there can be no consolation at the end of the lies. There is only failure, grief, and self-erasure. Behind the lies there's only the poet's pale, sick face. The mask, which is the poet's face, the face behind the mask, the poet endlessly looks back at the back of her head. There is only technique, rhetoric, parody, and paradox in order to hide the lies. Literature isn't sacred. It's a failure. Defeat. It's not a drawing made by language. Not even misery painted by language. Only that despair gives birth to technique.†
Despair invents ventriloquy.‡ No comfort can exist between the writer and the reader. Only the taut symmetrical world exists like the Yi Sang inside and outside of the mirror. The Yi Sang outside the mirror speaks for the Yi Sang inside the mirror. Ventriloquy. Strange though. The Yi Sang inside the mirror is more vivid. But the twins of the inside and outside of my mirror are playing jump rope. They'll endlessly give birth to twin families.

In my country, male poets rarely succeed at speaking in a woman's voice. The male poets who lived under the Japanese colonial occupation mostly wrote poetry through a female persona. Inside their poetry, the male poets acted like women and spoke with a woman's voice. Though they were living in a colony, they conveniently set up the colony inside their bellies. They comfortably fitted themselves with wombs, then took them off like bras. They automatically ventriloquized women whenever they were overcome with farewell, sorrow, loss, nation, racial identity, discontent, crisis, blame. To live out whatever little eros was left in them. To divulge their shameful desires. To resent the power that abandoned them. They needed the woman, the colony within, to express their natural desires, to realize their compassion and remorse. At the time, it was impossible for them as men to utter such

---

† Yi Sang, *Poetry and Fiction* (1936): "Despair gives birth to technique, and I fall once again into despair because of technique."
‡ Yi Sang, "The Story of a Big Dog" (Munhaksasang, July 1976): "Ventriloquism, ultimately, runs the storeroom of language."

emotions or desires. Literature was no different from the numerous pop song lyrics of farewell produced during the colonial period. The male poets longed for the women they parted from to live inside their hearts, to comfort them. They wanted the women to mourn on their behalf. Whenever gendered metaphors are used without technique, rhetoric, or camouflage of form, woman appears. When the ventriloquy ends, the woman is erased again. So, which one is the doll? Is it the man who is ventriloquizing or the woman hidden inside his belly? Or both? Or is it the real woman who remains silent outside of them?

That I live, that I continually experience. As a living organism, I interact with things that surround me. I have an animal body that's connected to the natural world, as well as to my body that imagines. The imaginary experience doesn't leave the sensory experience alone. Deformation begins. I think of Time as the "doing" of the imaginary experience. When Time intervenes, my sensory experience emerges as an irreducible shape. I write. As I write, as I begin the evocation, the continuity of the sensory and imaginary coheres. The binding force between the two becomes stronger. This is why, beyond time and space, Nature and I are inside the wholeness, inside the synergy. My imaginary experience becomes somatic. My body, unsevered from Nature, resides in what I call "a field-of-doing." My writing involves composing the field-of-doing. As in Yi Sang's line "ventriloquism, ultimately, runs the storeroom of language," my writing is the ventriloquy of the two experiences. Running the storeroom of language is my writing process.

Two birds flew by my kitchen window. The birds' necks were as thick as a human's. I could clearly see the bird flying in front, and the bird next to it looked blurry, but I could tell that they were of the same species. As the first bird flew near me, I saw its face. The bird had a human face. When I woke up from the dream, I knew my daddy would soon pass away. I don't know why I thought this. But it didn't occur to me then that the blurry bird was my mommy. Mommy passed away soon after Daddy. I was angry at myself for not asking why two birds had appeared in my dream. I felt as if my face had been buried in the sand. I came to write *Phantom Pain Wings* after Daddy passed away. I called out for birds endlessly. I wanted to become a translator of bird language. Bird language that flies to places I've never been. I went to Jeju Island and visited the 4.3 Museum.[§] I also went to an art gallery to look

---

§ On April 3, 1948, eighty thousand civilians on Jeju Island were massacred by South Korean and US troops in order to suppress the so-called communist uprising.

at paintings that depicted the massacre; then one evening, I spoke with an old woman who had survived the anti-communist slaughter. I recorded the old woman. I couldn't understand the dialect she was using, so I asked someone who worked at the café to translate what the old woman said. Everything she talked about concerned death. All kinds of death. That night in my dream, I saw birds hanging from a tree by their necks, like ribbons. I couldn't tell if the birds were alive or dead, but their feathers fluttered in the same direction. It looked as if the birds all had something to say. I kept having more bird dreams. If I didn't jot down my dreams, bird would fall from sky. I also thought of the ventriloquy of sky. Sky, ventriloquizing through the mouths of all living things. My breath enters the breath of the sky and speaks. Sky's breath enters mine and speaks. The more sky breaths enter the closer I am to death. I'm like a piece of paper the birds suspended in air stomp on, leaving their footprints. I think of the letter left by the dead tied around my neck. While I was writing *Phantom Pain Wings*, every morning when I opened my eyes, I felt as if I were trapped inside the two-dimensional paper. Or I felt as if I were water spreading and seeping into dirt, like a dead bird. When bird flew in to snatch a piece of paper with its beak, my blanket lifted, and I could sit up as in a three-dimensional world. It felt like bird was "doing" me.

After Mommy died, my trypophobia intensified. Now I can't stand seeing clusters of holes. I can't bring myself to open any containers filled with matchsticks, toothpicks, and cotton swabs. I refuse any dishes sprinkled heavily with sesame seeds. I have to close my eyes before them. So, when someone said, "Sesame seeds sprinkled on a wound," I wanted to strangle her. I can't bear looking at pipes stacked up on trucks, orderly decorative holes on the outer walls of buildings, or even soldiers marching in line. Photos of rows of people's heads taken from above. Now I can't even bring myself to read. When I open a book, the first thing I see are the holes of the consonant ㅇ.** Those little vacuous holes stare at me. Soon ㆆ †† consonants. Next are consonants ㅁ, ‡‡ then ㅂ. §§ I had no choice but to read books in English. But then I found "o's" in English. I begin to detest the letters "a," "b," "d," "p," "q" in this order. Also capital "Q" and "R." I can only read after I black out the letters with my pen. But there are still too many hole letters. The book eventually is

---

** ㅇ sounds like letter "e."
†† ㆆ sounds like letter "h."
‡‡ ㅁ sounds like letter "m."
§§ ㅂ sounds like letter "b."

completely blackened. I throw out poetry books filled with blackened letters. After Mommy dies, I fall into selective mutism once again.***

I erase the ㅇㅁㅁ consonants from 엄마 ŏmma [mommy] and leave only the ㅓ, ㅏ vowels. ㅓㅏ, ㅓㅏ, ㅓㅏ, ㅓㅏ, ㅓㅏ, ㅓㅏ, ㅓㅏ, ㅓㅏ, ㅓㅏ, ㅓ ㅏ, ㅓㅏ ††

Erased consonants look for me, or don't. What's found is the erased, so it's no better than not looking in the first place; the not-looking acknowledges the erased, so it's also no better than not looking. Therefore, I keep erasing until the erased consonants pat me, hug me, take me away, and speak to me. ㅇㅁㅁ, ㅇㅁㅁ, ㅇㅁㅁ, ㅇㅁㅁ ‡‡ the sound of Mommy crying from somewhere. The sound of me crying when I take myself away as I leave this world ㅇㅁㅁ, ㅇㅁㅁ, ㅇㅁㅁ. The sound of my real mommy crying.

Recently, in South Korea, those who have watched the report on TV about a sixteen-month-old baby who died after she was beaten are filled with rage. A young mother, who adopted the baby, abused her and killed her. The child's pancreas was found severed, and her abdomen was filled with blood. Watching the news made me depressed, and made me think of Bird Rider.§§§ Bird Rider is the spirit of a dead baby; shamans become possessed by it. Bird Rider is a baby ghost—rejected by its mother and starved, it becomes a ghost after it dies. Bird Rider channels its voice through the shaman, in the voice of a baby, but sometimes in the voice of a bird, chirping. Nobody understands the chirping. Another shaman must translate it. Sometimes the chirping doesn't come from the tip of Bird Rider's tongue but from the flowers in the yard. From the bubbling stream. From the swirling hand fan. When the village people want to catch a burglar, they call for Bird Rider. Because it can fly like a bird to the past and look down at the scene of a crime. At times, Bird Rider comes and speaks in the untranslatable fragmented language of the wounded. During the London Olympics, one poet from each country arrived at the Southbank Center. Two hundred poets took part in the Poetry Parnassus reading. The poets read in their own language while their poems in translation were projected onto the screen. Among them was a poet from Eritrea. She only made sounds of bird chirping with the tip of her tongue. Her

---

***   All the consonants blacked out have closed shapes. I don't erase open-shaped letters such as "c."

†††   ㅓ and ㅏ are vowels—they sound like "uh" and "ah."

‡‡‡   Whether you sound the consonants or the vowels separately in 엄마 ŏmma [mommy], they both sound like moans.

§§§   The name of baby ghost varies from province to province: 새타니 *Saetani*; 명도 *Myeongdo*; 태자 *Taeja*; 태자귀 *Taejagui*.

poem didn't need any translation on the screen. At that moment, I thought about the system called poetry. I breathed in deeply Bird Rider poet's voice outside the system.

The death of a family member, first of all, involves the sensation of a bodily separation. Everything around me testifies to the loss. Everything triggers the absence. My home has become an antique shop that sells absence. However, a departed bird always returns. Bird returns, carrying the essence of "the between" in its beak, to build its house in the terrain of dislocation, between the imaginary and the real, between language and reality. Bird isn't an imaginary suture of the gaps. It's not a phantom. Bird is a mechanism that subjectifies the gaps. Bird is a subject in process, making me give birth to the dead. The pain of mourning looks like the pain of childbirth. Through bird I give birth to Time that's mixed from existence and absence, with and without. Mourning doesn't stop. It fails. I don't write "about" bird; instead, I "do" bird. When I open my mouth, bird peers out from my mouth. I'm halfbird-halfhuman. I'm the subject as well as the object of my sentence. But, every day, before I can even complete a single line, dead bird falls from the sky.

Literary ventriloquy is not about imitation, but entanglement, impregnation of one another. My belly's internal soliloquy of I-do-animal. Reaching the extremity of imaginary experience via the internal soliloquy. I-do-somatization is woven with I-do-imagination. I-do-somatization triggers chronic illness like the shaman spirit-illness. At the height of grief, a frightening illness arrives as if I've felt the bird living inside me. Poet is unable to stand alone, facing infinity without going through sickness and pain. Such aberration is the beginning of the emergence of a doppelganger. It's an escape to the outside, from the human, surrendering one's body to the animal. Paradoxically, the aberrancy collects the sights of outside and sinks inside, endlessly. During my incessant inner travel, I reach the impersonality of the subject. At that place, the borderless place of life and death, I find my mommy, the dead child of my lost self. Upon visiting that place, I'm diseased, impaired, deformed. I'm animal pulled out from the inner sinking and extremity of X-ray vision. I make bird soar up the sky. The ruins of ingredients that made me. From there, from the bottom of the bottom, from the brink of becoming Other, from the mental breakdown, I need to haul up the voice that makes a bird's cry. This voice is my Other. I can't see it with my naked eye, but I've met it with my whole body. My Other used to live inside the mirror in front of me. Like the shaman's channeling, for my Other to speak, it needs my rhythm. It needs my breathing. While I write, I become an empty palanquin, carrying my Other. I become anonymous. I'll say it again, this isn't imitation.

It's the movement of my body, sending the ghost of extremity to its original place, to its inherent existential place, to my whole body. Jumping up and down, the ecstasy of rhythm and the dance come into my aid. As if wings are sprouting from my limbs. As if disobeying my existence. As if arriving at the ocean. Shaman's flagpoles shake very slowly or very fast, and bird soars up amidst the frenzied clanging of gongs. Bird flies up from the height of inner confinement the way Bird Rider begins bird ventriloquy. The existence and the other embrace, as twins, inside my belly, like when Bird Rider's channeling of voice is about to explode. But their time of flight is near. It's time for them to fly up high like drones and point out the place of the thievery to the village people. Wit, irony, and paradox dance wildly. I utter every word in two overlapping voices. Self-proliferation begins.

—*Kim Hyesoon*
Seoul, February 4, 2021

Translator's Diary

JANUARY 10

Double S / Double S: Kim Hyesoon (KH) deploys a double consonant ㅆ. Sonically, the letter "s" is close to the single consonant ㅅ. Hence, ㅆ = ss. They are the birds' webbed feet, poet and bird swaddled as one. In 2019, I emailed Kim the draft translation of the poem. She said it made her laugh.

JANUARY 12

Phantom Pain Wings: In Korean the words for 세 = rent and 새 = bird are homonyms. I opted for "bird house" because it made me think of KH's tiny rental writing studio. You really have to be a bird to fit into it. In 2018, I had the privilege of peeping into the room when she invited me, Jeffrey Yang, and Christopher Mattison to her secret bird house. She posed for us, sitting at her desk, smiling, below a birdcage-sized window.

JANUARY 18

Back to revising ***Phantom Pain Wings***. I had a difficult time figuring out what and who the subject was in the poem. In Korean, things still make sense without stating the subject. Such lack of specificity or subjectivity creates space for much ambiguity and delay in clarity about the subject or even object of the sentence. When I asked KH who the speaking subject was, she answered, "I wrote it in a way that bird = I is speaking. In other words, the speaker is a bird-human. Bird-human is the 'I.'" And regarding 그들 = they, which suddenly appears, I translated as "critics." KH later confirmed for me that she was referring to those who didn't understand her poem "I'm OK, I'm Pig!" from her collection *Bloom, Pig* (2016), which was chosen for the 5.18 Gwangju Literature Award. (5.18 refers to the Gwangju Uprising, which began on May 18, 1980, when civilians and students were massacred by the military troops.) Her critics in Gwangju vehemently opposed this award. KH declined the award.

Grief Guitar: Once again, I wasn't clear about who the speaking subject was when KH used 서로 = each other and 우리 = we/our. I first asked KH about this on May 24, 2020. She explained that the guitarist is referring to his/her guitar as 너 = you. And therefore, the guitar becomes a person, and so the guitarist and you become each other/we/our. She had once seen a dance performance inside an old coal mine. "The poem is trying to say what a guitarist (poet) of South Korea is doing and can do." Since KH pointed out that the "dancers" could also be part of "each other/we/our," I decided to spell all of them out, especially because the Korean transliterated word for guitar = 기타 is the same as the Korean word for 기타 = etcetera.

Girl, Your Body Has So Many Holes for Straws: In line three, the original translates as "escape from time"—what is escaping from time is not indicated. KH answered on May 21, 2020: "What I thought of first was a bird that is tied to a piano string, a bird that can fly up to white beard's shop. Like my poem, that's the limit of bird's freedom. Next, I thought why should there be just one persona/speaker in a poem? So I wanted I, bird, and music to all speak. The three are speaking in unison." Then KH proposed the idea of "I = bird (tied up with a piano strong) = music." Later, we agreed to use the plus sign instead for the multiple personas/speakers. KH added, "It's uplifting to answer your questions. For an entire year, I thought of nothing but my mom." Her mother passed away in 2019.

Crow's Eye View 31: KH uses Yi Sang's given name, Kim Haekyeong. This poem is a parody of Yi Sang's poem "Poem No. 1" from a series "Crow's Eye View." "Wings" (1936) is one of Yi Sang's best known short stories:

> Suddenly my armpits itch. Ah, the marks left behind where my artificial wings had sprouted. Today, I'm wingless.

I became befuddled by the lines about birds flying because when I was a child ("I'm still the 13th child" as I stated in *Hardly War*), I often heard grown-ups use an expression in the context of what was going on with the government under the dictatorship—"so and so's neck flew away," which means that someone got fired. The Korean words for "get fired" and "fly away" are the same, which may or may not explain my befuddlement. When I asked KH about this, she replied: "Our country has governed its citizens by invoking fear of North Korea. So then we all end up following one terrified bird and fly, terrified. This is why I used the word 'nation'."

JANUARY 23

A cold, sunny day. Snow expected at sea level this coming week.

Birds' Funeral: KH gave me two copies of *Phantom Pain Wings*. One clean signed copy and the other with some notes for me in Korean and English. Beside this poem, she wrote in English "funeral speech" so that I wouldn't confuse it with other homonyms. She also suggested in English "suddenlybird." She noted "quiet" next to Korean onomatopoeia for "shh." In Korean it sounds like "shht." All other wordplays in the poem I carried over into English, sonically speaking. Translating KH's bird language is unsettling. I think it's also the most difficult language of KH's so far.

JANUARY 24

I woke up early again feeling anxious about everything. An email from Sasha Dugdale in England: "I have been working slowly on Keats and feeling rather down. As you've probably heard (like the US) we are losing so many lives here and it definitely affects everyone."

JANUARY 25

Again, I Need to Ask Poor Yi Sang: "Crazy bastard's nonsense, what bullshit, kill him!" This is in reference to some insults thrown at Yi Sang when his experimental serial poem "Crow's Eye View" was published in *Chosun Central Daily*, 1934. "surkoreanpoemaordojunta" is very likely to be a parody of the Korean Writers Association. I believe KH is recalling the insults against Yi Sang in reference to the ones thrown at her when her book was selected as the winner of the 5.18 Gwangju Literature Award. From "I'm OK, I'm Pig!" (Action Books, 2014):

Boars come and tear into the pigs
A flock of eagles comes and tears into the pigs

Night of internal organs raining down from the sky!
Night of flashing decapitated pigs!
Fearful night, unable to discard Pig even if I die and die again!
Night filled with pig squeals from all over!

Night of screams, I'm Pig! Pig!

Night when pigs bloom dangling-dangling from the pig-tree

JANUARY 29

Portrait of Fear: This might be extremely boring to some, but I used long dashes in order to replicate the rhythm of the Korean syntax in which the subject appears at the end of the sentence repeatedly.

To add to the boredom, I did something similar in "Bird's Poetry Book" on page 11 by hyphenating the words:

Bird-carrying-the-night's-nipple-
over-the-pointed-as-an-awl-Mount-Everest sequence

. . .

The tiny bird's
kicks-off-the-blanket-kicks-my-body-
kicks-the-dirt-and-exits sequence

Once again, I wanted to replicate the syntax in Korean, not that this makes things better or more interesting in English. It's just that it's one more possibility, one more language.

Mailbox: Mailboxes in South Korea are red. I think of the red mailbox as the organ of parting in the book. This whole second section of the book reads like a fairy tale about parting.

Filling Out Customs Forms on the Last Day of the Month: I've become so fond of "postwoman" and her "dictionary of sea language." I wish I could get hold of her dictionary and use it to translate KH's bird language, language of parting, her "mirror-like words." Many years ago, I took a postal exam. Everyone turned around to look at me when I said that I didn't have a green card. Maybe I looked like one of the girls from the ocean then.

Candle: *Our Joyful Days of Youth* (1987) is the title of a Korean film. KH wrote in her book for me that "When someone sobbing gets in the face of / another sobber, igniting in tears" is a scene of one candle lighting another. Those familiar with South Korean boy or girl bands may not need an explanation for the Korean word *oppa*—girls or women use it to address their older brothers. It is now commonly used to refer to one's boyfriend or any older male. KH has previously parodied *oppa* in her poem "Double *p*–How Creepy" in *All the Garbage of the World, Unite!* (Action Books, 2011):

> Two of my married former students showed up with their husbands and one called her husband *oppa* and the other called her husband pappa—how creepy. I had no choice but to say, I'm leaving first. I can't bear to hear any more of this kinship name nonsense. I'm so afraid of *pp* that I don't want to say happy or cute.

JANUARY 29

It felt like a birthday. Deborah Woodard, a poet and translator friend, dropped off some KN95 masks, two cans of tuna, two bars of chocolate, a jar of blackberry spread, and hibiscus tea. Deborah says she's where I'm at with her revision work of *Documento* (1976) by Amelia Rosselli. Deborah has been, for the past twenty years or more, translating Rosselli's experimental anti-fascist poetry. We have exchanged poems and translations every Saturday for many years. But now, it doesn't matter which day it is.

JANUARY 30

In my dream I kept stuttering. I wasn't even trying to say anything particularly important. How pathetic. I don't know which is worse—having anxiety in dreams or in waking life. Just the other day, I thought all the birds in my yard had died, but today I see towhees and juncos at the feeder hanging from the old apple tree.

JANUARY 31

Little Poem: KH creates a wordplay by listing a string of words that sound similar to "clean," which sounds similar to "shit" in English. Hence, I end the wordplay with "shhit shhit shhit." This translingual wordplay does indeed change the meaning of clean to "shhit," but not the larger meaning or tone of the poem. It's just another way the littleness can resist the bigness.

Postwoman: In the third stanza, KH lists Korean postpositions without any spaces:

은는이가	isareambe
을를에의	inonatof
와과만도	andwithonlytoo

The particles I chose are not exactly equivalent to Kim's because equivalents are not easy to come by in my translation universe. They're somewhat approximate while also very different than the postwoman who is "nothing like the glasses the deceased are wearing." This to me is one of the genius characteristics of Kim's poetry. Her nothingness and littleness eventually pile up to topple things— to topple power, I mean. So it's no surprise that my universe is also filled with littleness and nothingness. I'm reminded of the lines from "I'll Call Those Things My Cats" in *Poor Love Machine* (Action Books, 2016):

> These adorable things. When my life gives out, they'd eat me up in a second. When it rains, they make me drag a leather sofa outdoors. They even build houses inside my nostrils. They'd even devour my elephant. They are like the stars that can't be seen in daylight.

Grammatical particles, adorable or not, are always torturous to me. They require another kind of dictionary, not only tiny in size, but the user of the dictionary also has to be tiny enough to use it. Is this why people say translators are invisible? Although, I do love hiding. Little things usually do. While I was in Berlin, I was invisible to everyone, even dogs, except little children, as if I had entered the world of *The Wings of Desire*. It felt glamorous to be invisible. In Seoul, the only ones who can see me are older men. One said as he passed me, "Hey lady, your sunglasses are too dark." How creepy!

JANUARY 31

438,035 COVID-19 deaths in the US; 2,236,035 worldwide.

I revisited Sasha's editorial in *The Great Flight: Refugee Focus* issue of *Modern Poetry in Translation* (2016):

> And what can we do, except to continue to believe in our own form of the Republic of Letters . . . a virtual and metaphysical utopia where poets of all races and places meet and share poetry? It's a minute and fragile vision. . . .

And an interview I did with KH in *Autobiography of Death* (New Directions, 2018):

> Why does our country make us ashamed for being alive, for surviving those tragic events? . . . I came to think that I, we are all part of the structure of death, that we remain living in it.
>
> . . .
>
> And I thought to myself that I needed to excavate the faceless face with language, excavate the face with the rhythm embodied in language. I came to think more fervently than ever that someone involved in such idle labor is a poet.

Little translators know how to maintain a minute and fragile vision by performing the utopic idle labor within the structure of death, through our day-to-day, inconsequential living.

FEBRUARY 1

The witch hazel outside the window is in full bloom.

Pointed Handwriting: In the stanza before the last, KH utilizes words that begin with 숲 = forest and words that begin with 수 (without the ㅍ). Therefore, I thought it might work best to generate words conjoined with forest:

> "Forest, my forestbird, my forestSufism, my forestdeity."

FEBRUARY 2

KH sent a large box of KF94 masks. I love that they are individually wrapped. I can't help being a nationalist when it comes to masks.

FEBRUARY 4

A nuthatch has returned.

FEBRUARY 6

In the second section of the book, COMMUNITY OF PARTING, an epic ontological, existential poem, KH circled the words 작별 which appear in the title of the section and subtitle, "Body of Parting," and penciled in English, "parting."

Another word she wrote for me in English was 파리, which sounds very close to the French pronunciation of Paris = 파리 = pale.

When I was learning English in Hong Kong, I loved saying "yeah" instead of "yes" because "yeah" almost sounds like the polite form of "yes" (예) in Korean. So I couldn't help being offended when people thought that my 예~ ("yeah") was improper when I was being extra polite, as always.

Bird's Diary: "Go! Go!" in Korean is 가가, which sounds like "ga ga." I adore proximities of sounds across vast linguistic distances. It's like meeting my long-lost twin.

Winter Solstice Recipe: My mother used to make red-bean porridge for us on winter solstice. She also pressed pine nuts for oil that she lit as a lamp during the night. She gave me and my siblings whole walnuts, and we rubbed the shells together to make them shine. In Hong Kong, my mother was perpetually disappointed with how the red beans tasted. I disliked beans as a child, so I only missed the walnuts.

Is There White Light for Us?: "Jesus, Mommy's Jesus, you raise up so many lilies" refers to the line in the hymn "The Lily of the Valley": "He's the Lily of the Valley, the Bright and Morning Star."

FEBRUARY 7

I revised "lilyasphyxiating" to "lilyphyxiating." From now on if anyone asks me what my translation approach is, I'll say, "Lilymethod."

Shredded Bird: "Bloom, Pig!" is from the poem "I'm OK, I'm Pig":

Has to die even if it didn't steal
Has to die even if it didn't kill
Without a trail
Without a whipping
Has to go into the pit to be buried

. . .

A horde of healthy pigs like strong young men gets thrown into the pit

They cry in the grave
They cry standing on two legs, not four
They cry with dirt over their heads
It's not that I can't stand the pain!

It's the shame!
Inside the grave, stomachs fill with broth, broth and gas
Stomachs burst inside the grave

They boil up like a crummy stew
Blood flows out the grave
On a rainy night fishy-smelling pig ghosts flash flash
Busted intestine tunnel their way up from the grave and soar above the
    mound
A resurrection! Intestine is alive! Like a snake!

Bloom, Pig!

FEBRUARY 10

Tomorrow is the lunar new year. I emailed KH, and KH emailed me back. When we began emailing about twenty years ago, she instructed me to always write her name in the subject line.

Sadly, I fell asleep during Brenda Hillman's lecture on "Metaphor and Metonymy." I'm not sure when I drifted off. When I woke up, she was talking about having a problem with one of her eyes and how it induces visual hallucinations.

I remember reading something KH wrote about her refusal of metaphors—metaphors predetermined by male poets for women, metaphors that uphold patriarchy. Deborah says that "she doesn't need metaphors because she generates complete and utter metamorphoses."

FEBRUARY 11

Just before I woke up, I dreamt about how I should write about the student who self-immolated himself and jumped from the Seoul National University building in 1986. It was a protest-suicide to raise awareness about the Gwangju massacre. I wondered how many times he might have fainted while falling into the funnel of his own flames.

I remember a nightmare I had in January. I don't remember the date. My sister bit my hand. The look of her teeth scared me more than the pain.

Snow flurries outside.

FEBRUARY 13

I see fat snowflakes.

Adverbs, Fly: Koreans never address their fathers or daddys with a pronoun 너 "you," which is only reserved for someone younger or below in social standing than oneself, or during friendly banters with one's peers. But KH addresses her daddy as "you" throughout the poem. She may have broken the most sacred decorum of Korean language.

FEBRUARY 14

I see witch hazel yellow blossoms covered in snow.

Red Bean Handstand: On November 6, 2020, KH replied to my question about "Jung-yeob": "It's the name of a Korean artist, Jung Jung-yeob. She draws and paints everything such as the moon, jars, and masses with beans. . . . Once, in 1992, we traveled together to Angkor Wat, Cambodia. She told me that she threw her bag down and hid it, so she could secretly leave the house and go on the trip with me. She loved traveling and hiking so much that she used to hike alone at night on the trails of Taebaek and Jiri mountains. She's daring."

I think KH might have traveled to Angkor Wat a second time because one summer, perhaps ten years ago, she sent me a photo of herself in front of a temple relic totally entangled in snake-like tree roots.

My father once told me that the most beautiful place he had been to in his life was Angkor Wat. He was dispatched to Laos and Cambodia during the Secret War. I vaguely remember that my mother was in a perpetual state of crisis while we lived in Hong Kong.

It's still snowing outside. I'm still the 13th child. In reality, we were all motherless.

A Blizzard Warning: I thought I should add these Korean endings ㅆㅆ ㅆㅆ ㅆㅆ as in the original. These are visual puns. (In "I'm OK, I'm Pig!" Kim uses number 9 as a pig's tail: "Pig9.") They are shapes of trousers, hand-holding, wings, sprouts. ㅆ also sounds similar to "shit." Hence "Shitty word endings." Double ㅅ is used for a past tense ending: ㅆ = ed. She also uses other words with double ㅅ: 쌍쌍이 = in pairs; 싹들 = sprouts; 쓰라리라 = feel hurt; 불쌍하고 쓸쓸한 = poor, lonely. Kim Hyesoon wrote on the page in English "~ed" and "d d d d." This marker "~" is a perfect bird language translation formula.

I see Kim Hyesoon's father's and my father's ㅆㅆ ㅆㅆ ㅆㅆ—trousers or wings, holding hands across wars.

FEBRUARY 16

I found a twin image of the falling student. For the Exploratory Translation Colloquium, Jen Scappettone gave a short introduction about the image of a falling figure from the Tower of Babel in the Bedford Hours (c. 1410–30) that she used as her background screen for the online event: "fall . . . dive . . . many ways to fall . . . fall is multidirectional . . . more diving . . . multipolarity."

FEBRUARY 20

I saw a cyclone formation in my dream. It looked exactly like an atomic bomb cloud. In fact, I had to reassure myself that it was a cyclone and not the bomb. Then I watched the arrows of air currents rising and falling. I knew in the dream that I was dreaming about Kim Hyesoon's cyclone poem *Tyrannus Melancholicus* (See p. 54).

FEBRUARY 22

Another nightmare. People were casually lounging on a sofa next to each other, barely six feet apart, without any masks on.

FEBRUARY 23

500,000 COVID deaths in the US; 2,411,877 worldwide.

Chorus: I translated the lines from the Korean translation of "Ode to Joy" KH used in the poem.

MARCH 2

Bragging About My Dress: KH pointed out to me the three lines that begin with "The saying that . . ." are based on Korean proverbs:

"When a hen crows three times, the entire household will be ruined"; "Women and dried fish need to be beaten three times a day in order to make them tasty"; "Plates break when three women get together." I grew up hearing these proverbs frequently, as they were used by women against other women.

Several poems in WHY DO WOMEN THINK THAT ANIMALS CAN SPEAK? depict abuse against women and children. It's interesting that even Sylvia Plath makes an appearance in one of the poems, *The Stretcher*.

March feels doomed. My mother called to say my father lost his balance and fell flat on his face.

MARCH 3

Beneath the dark cover of the cart / splendid coffins made of ebony / are swiftly dragged by the strong mares / with shiny dark-blue hair: These lines are from "Ornières" in *Illuminations* by Arthur Rimbaud. I translated them from the Korean translation KH used.

MARCH 5

Autism, 1000: KH's footnote for the poem reads: From Diego Velázquez's "Portrait of Pope Innocent X" emerges Francis Bacon's "Study after Velazquez's Portrait of Pope Innocent X" and from Bacon's "Study after Velazquez's Portrait of Pope Innocent X" emerges my "innocent" pope.

Perhaps the teeth dream I had in January came from this poem.

MARCH 6

During my walk I spotted a long-white-eyebrowed wren.

MARCH 16

STOP AAPI HATE has received reports of 3,795 hate incidents from March 19, 2020 to February 28, 2021. This day, eight people were shot at massage parlors in Atlanta. Six of the killed were Asian women.

The translation of *Phantom Pain Wings* was supported by a grant from the Literature Translation Institute of Korea.

Thank you to the editors of the journals in which some of the poems have previously appeared: *Astra, Boston Review, Chicago Review, INQUE Magazine, Michigan Quarterly Review, Spoon River Review, The Nation, The New York Times Magazine,* and *Washington Square Review.*

My deep gratitude to Deborah Woodard, Kim Hyesoon, Jeffrey Yang, and everyone at New Directions.

—Don Mee Choi
Seattle, 2021

KIM HYESOON, one of the most influential contemporary poets in South Korea, is the author of several books of poetry and essays. She has received many awards for her poetry, including the 2019 International Griffin Poetry Prize for *Autobiography of Death* (New Directions, 2018) and the prestigious Samsung Ho-Am Prize in 2022. Besides English, Kim's work has been translated into Chinese, Danish, French, German, Japanese, Spanish, and Swedish.

DON MEE CHOI's *DMZ Colony* (Wave Books, 2020) received a National Book Award for Poetry. She is a recipient of fellowships from the MacArthur, Guggenheim, Lannan, and Whiting Foundations, as well as the DAAD Artists-in-Berlin Program.